THROWING MOSES UNDER THE BUS

*T*hrowing *M*oses under the *B*us

A HIGH SCHOOL ENGLISH TEACHER
LOOKS AT THE TEN COMMANDMENTS

John Cabascango

RESOURCE *Publications* • Eugene, Oregon

THROWING MOSES UNDER THE BUS
A High-School English Teacher Looks at the Ten Commandments

Copyright © 2019 John Cabascango. All rights reserved. Except for brief quotations in critical publications or reviews, no part of this book may be reproduced in any manner without prior written permission from the publisher. Write: Permissions, Wipf and Stock Publishers, 199 W. 8th Ave., Suite 3, Eugene, OR 97401.

Resource Publications
An Imprint of Wipf and Stock Publishers
199 W. 8th Ave., Suite 3
Eugene, OR 97401

www.wipfandstock.com

PAPERBACK ISBN: 978-1-5326-9563-6
HARDCOVER ISBN: 978-1-5326-9564-3
EBOOK ISBN: 978-1-5326-9565-0

Manufactured in the U.S.A.   AUGUST 29, 2019

For Esteban

Contents

Introduction | ix

Chapter One	First Things	1
Chapter Two	God Makers	11
Chapter Three	What Did You Say?	24
Chapter Four	Working Ourselves to Death	29
Chapter Five	Mom, Dad and the You, You Can't See	34
Chapter Six	The Most Obvious Commandment, Sort Of...	42
Chapter Seven	The Other Commandment Everyone Knows and Tells Stories About	46
Chapter Eight	The Commandment We Quibble Over the Most	55
Chapter Nine	The Easiest Commandment to Break?	62
Chapter Ten	When It All Comes Together	68
Chapter Eleven	Moving Forward, Wrapping Up	73

Introduction

TALKING about the Ten Commandments (hereafter referred to only as the Commandments) is dangerous business. Perhaps that's because so many people have an opinion about them and very few Americans can list them. Before Judge Roy Moore's senate run, he gained fame attempting to have the Commandments used as a monument of sorts to acknowledge what he said was a higher authority. Originally, the monument was of wood and hung on a wall. By the time the controversy made its move to the State Supreme Court of Alabama, the monument was a 5,280-pound monument of stone that even a Marvel Comics version of Moses would have struggled to carry down the mountain. Still, the size and, more specifically, the weight of the monument are both ironic and telling in its lack of portability and its deeply locational relevance. It's as if Alabama had become the location of traditional morality, and the weight of the monument made sure the Commandments weren't going to travel easily. Years later, Judge Moore, after several failed political runs, was discredited in the wake of sexual conduct accusations, which were deeply disturbing. Still, the issue of the Commandments and moral law once played a major role in any a public discussion of behavior but now is more of a red flag likely to get one dismissed as politically extreme or just generally narrow-minded and intolerant. In *Stone v. Graham*, the posting of the Commandments in public-school classrooms was found to be against the First Amendment because it had no secular

INTRODUCTION

base.¹ As a result, the plaques being purchased by private funds were deemed irrelevant. So, here's where I and, more specifically, this book come in. Allow me to introduce myself with the specific goal of defining what the purpose of this book is and why I have any business writing it. First of all, I am not a lawyer nor have I ever lived in the state of Alabama. So there is no particular legal, geographical, or state-specific cultural reason for me to attempt writing about the Commandments. I have degrees from Wheaton College, a Christian College in Illinois. However, despite an integrated double major, which included Biblical Studies, I have no formal training in ancient languages. I was fortunate to add thirty-three hours of undergraduate Biblical Studies to my English major but make no claim to ancient linguistic competency, much less expertise. Personally, when asked to refer to myself as a Christian, at some points in the past, I would awkwardly admit to claiming the belief systems of an evangelical. The past few years of American politics have for the most part removed that label from my admitted identity, though one-on-one conversation will still bring me around to evangelical beliefs. I still hold that real conversion is possible and that, though it ought to be held compassionately, it is at times exclusive. I have regularly read and studied the Bible for most of my life. I was raised Southern Baptist but am the son of a somewhat lapsed Catholic father and a devout Southern Baptist mother. I have attended church regularly my whole life though I stopped attending Baptist churches sometime in my early twenties largely due to political and social reasons. Despite reading and memorizing various parts of scripture, I still have to be intentional about remembering the Commandments. Now, with that fairly harmless self-disclosure out of the way, I bring myself to the reason for this book—specifically that I am a veteran high-school teacher finishing up my twenty-first year of teaching high school and my seventeenth year of working in the public-school system. My own faith and lack thereof push me to reexamine how to communicate truth and often place me in the somewhat intellectually marginal area of trying to figure out how to express something

1. Robinson, Malila N. Encyclopedia Britannica. *Stone v. Graham.*

INTRODUCTION

simultaneously close to my heart and publicly awkward or even embarrassing. As far as the Commandments are concerned, I have no desire to post them in the halls of my school, in large part, because politicizing the sacred usually pushes people away from actual practiced belief. Besides, most things on the wall are ignored or vandalized in relatively socially accepted ways. Also, my first reflex is to look at the way teenagers interpret things and see it as the most obvious of interpretations, adolescent ones. The adolescent way of looking at things is connected to those who work with them, underpaid rescuers, or those who might struggle with cynicism from trying to save those who are convinced they don't need saving or that they can do a better job than all the adults who just don't understand. This might be a formula for interpreting the Commandments in the worst possible ways. Well, if you watch the nightly news, it isn't hard to argue that the world is not the way it should be. So instead of arguing for the reality of original sin or some more politically correct way of saying the world has a bent toward the screwed up, I'm going just to assume it. Also, I'm going to assume that the world can identify that it is having problems but doesn't like the cost of redemption and the moral boundaries that go with it. The physical metaphor would be living with cancer or even diabetes; those diagnosed with either or both need to live disciplined lives, if they desire to live. The consequences for them if they choose to step outside the boundaries of what is healthy or refuse proper treatment are fatal. I don't intend to argue this extensively but will assume it throughout the book.

Another assumption I will make is that although most people with high-school diplomas in the United States graduated from the public-school system, most of our problems regarding moral boundaries reflect the inability of people to move out of adolescence into adulthood. Further, I will also assume that adolescence is not just a one-time stage of development but a moral place where even the most responsible and committed adults fall back into when under stress or some other personal or public pitfall. So, if this work at times falls back on what seems basic or even shallow, that is less of a reflection on the Commandments themselves

INTRODUCTION

and more on the juvenile nature of people in the United States. Are people juvenile in other cultures? Pretty much, but I'll speak from where I live and move outward. Unlike the monument in the state of Alabama, I'm going to assume that the Commandments were something to be carried around, weighty in their reality but imminently portable. I will also assume that moral law exists with or without our knowledge and that breaking those laws brings consequences, with or without our understanding. If this seems unfair to some, my arguments may never bridge the "fairness" gap because moral law can work like gravity, whether one acknowledges it or not. And just like gravity, those who understand it and the consequences and rewards connected to it may benefit but can certainly take no credit for its existence. Since I am an English teacher, most of my commentary will come from narratives I have both read and taught as well as what I would call hallway commentary. By this, I mean the daily revelations that come from watching and interacting with high-school students. Of course, my classroom interactions are also part of the presentations, but the more obvious and more natural points are made from the rawer aspects of human nature, of which the public-school hallway is a raw, dark example.

I need to include a brief word here about the types I will use to examine the Commandments and how we relate to them. Of course, there are stereotypes, and all stereotypes can be argued away based on one exception. I'm not sure if I want to say that the people I will refer to are archetypes, but that would be more helpful in that the categories and patterns they call to mind are recognizable but not all inclusive. I bring this up to avoid having to clutter each point with qualifications over who is or isn't and what's fair or unfair. So, despite what might seem a heavy, droll subject, I invite you to take another look at the Ten Commandments and how they still relate to our society and ourselves.

Chapter One

First Things

I am the Lord your God who brought you out of Egypt, out of the land of slavery. Therefore you shall have no other gods before me.

—EXOD. 20:2-3

FRAULEIN Maria once said, "Let's start at the very beginning, a very good place to start." That being said the context of the Commandments is quite obviously the Exodus, people freed from slavery. Egypt is where they've come from, and the commands are why they owe God their loyalty, even their worship. However, what was Egypt? Very simply, without writing a tome on Egyptian history, Egypt was the global superpower of the day. Egypt was the wealthiest, most powerful, and most technologically advanced civilization of its time—specifically, hundreds of years' worth of power and wealth. As is the nature of wealthy ancient powers, much of the work was done by slaves. Of course, that sort of abuse of power and wealth has faded as our technological advances and wealth have made us more benevolent. OK, OK, that critique is a bit too obvious. However, the condition remains and is part of the first command. If God is the deliverer and slavery is what they were delivered from, then that's why the Commandments are given. True, the inference is that the laws given are for free people, but this is as simple as the prohibition against having other gods. In fact, in a twenty-three English translation parallel, there is no functional difference in the words other than bondage versus slavery. In verse three, the difference is not sharp, but the verse has been translated as "no other gods but me," "no other gods before me," and "no other gods besides me".[1] The second obvious conclusion is that there were many gods. Don't put them before me is more of a commitment to monogamy in worship than an argument over the reality or unreality of the other gods. So, the immediate connection is that leaving Egypt meant leaving other gods and following the Commandments means having just one God, or at least one above others. The second possibility seems the most practical, as the ancient world was filled with deities and hierarchy. An ultimatum of this nature fulfills an almost marriage vow type of condition. It also seems reasonable to connect the plurality of worship with material wealth, since Egypt was the wealthier and more powerful of the two cultures mentioned in the opening verses. So, if the new condition of freedom comes with conditions, then freedom isn't free (to borrow a well-used cliché). The newly freed people are given a choice of allegiance before they are given choices in general. This is more problematic for the average person than it might originally seem because such a demand is a swapping of masters and could be seen as simply switching slave positions. Well, instead of trying to nuance my way through that statement, I think it is more honest to simply state that the text is a swapping of masters with the promise of freedom: many masters are swapped with one. Freedom isn't our adolescent desire to simply do what we want but is a choice to submit to that which makes us free. It's probably not hard to see the usual adolescent response to such a claim. That seems unfair! If I'm free, why should I have so many rules? Don't you trust me? That sort of immediate challenge leads to many complaints throughout the Exodus narrative, most of which are accompanied by descriptions of melons and other treats the ancient Hebrews had while they were in slavery. It is important to remember here that Biblical freedom isn't opposed to treats or

1. Biblestudytools.com/compare-translations/exodus/20/

other pleasures, but these pleasures are not dangled out in front of us as some sort of tasty carrot. The bluntness of focus is simple: you were a slave, and now you're not. To better understand this command and our adolescent responses, it is best to introduce and explain two familiar characters. First is the high-school overachiever and the rebel without a cause. Many times, it is easier to start with the negative, so why fight it? Meet Pete the Pothead, the kid whose reading level is actually pretty high and who has had multiple teachers brand him with the worst of labels "potential." It isn't so much that Pete doesn't have potential, but that the more you repeat the word, the more it works as a curse, hammering home missed opportunities and lack of discipline. The truth is Pete could be a good student and can debunk most honor roll students in class debates, but Pete doesn't buy anything regarding incentives or arguments and as a result prefers the bathroom, nearby park, or wherever is most convenient to escape to feel better with whatever weed he can acquire. Pete sees the big picture regarding the logical fallacies and lousy promises presented by adults as incentives. He also sees the thin veneer of achievement masquerading as concern from his high-achieving peers. If Pete were in ancient Egypt, he could have been several characters: the cynical slave who works hard enough not to get whipped or the mid-ranking soldier or courtier who sees the intrigue of Pharaoh's more ambitious servants and officers but avoids catastrophe by maintaining loyalties as convenient to his station. He would observe and be able to name all the gods and would probably believe in none of them. Herein lies one of the great myths of the public-school system and many other large redemptive organizations. Yes, I said "redemptive" because that is its purpose—if not always, its measured, quantified end. But I digress. The first great myth to discuss is that many options bring about good choices. So, what does that have to do with the first commandment and our intelligent, albeit unmotivated, weed imbiber. Simply put, when many good options are unrealistically presented as more than they are, some people, like Pete, will see through the smoke screen and stop believing. These options for good when, unrealistically and constantly, elevated above what they truly are, can become false promises. In the ancient world, false promises were referred to as false prophecies, and the objects held up as offering false redemption were referred to by the ancient Hebrews as false gods. So maybe Pete is smart, maybe even smarter than many of the students around him. However, does his intelligence automatically bring back a dad who left and never came back years ago? Will his "potential" cure his mother of anxiety that makes her seem distant even as she seems likeable at the first interview? Probably not, and all the promises he receives from well-meaning teachers and counselors can be boiled down to money from a better job that is expected to be acquired as a result of getting an education. The ancient Egyptians had a lot more stuff than the ancient Hebrews. This was true before, during, and after slavery and didn't escape those who would have turned back to slavery because of the leeks and melons. Hey, it's in the text, and it meant more to them than to us (or at least those of us who don't like leeks). To a kid like Pete, or the adult he will become, caring about things in an exclusive manner is only valuable if he gets something out of it. The marijuana might go away and come back as an antidepressant, or the sluggishness might even be replaced by a drive for succeeding financially. One thing is certain: feeling better quickly can become feeling numb if feeling better doesn't last, as it seldom does in a world of too many options. Too many redemptive options don't have to lead to self-medicated cynicism; it could lead to overachievement.

This brings us to Patricia, the overachiever. She is not only a cynic but also buys into all the options. She is the head of multiple clubs, captain of one or two teams, volunteers in the community in ways no one would question and may even hold down a job. If you haven't guessed yet, her grades are solid, pushing her forward to what most systems would promise success and happiness. If Patricia were an ancient Egyptian, she would no doubt never miss an offering and would have all ceremonies timed on her sundial and mythological calendar of cosmic rewards. Patricia may at once have been social with or even friends with Pete, but she doesn't run in the same circles as he does. She runs circles around anyone who slows down, with or without chemical assistance. Patricia might be a member of the local church youth group, no doubt in good standing there, as well as in anything else she is involved in. As for stress, Patricia knows it and occasionally succumbs to it, with tears of fear and anguish over not being able to do everything well. The ancient Egyptians had all sorts of gods who required multiple sacrifices. The keyword is "sacrifice," and that is not painless. In fact, most of the time something dies in the process. Whereas Pete died inside somewhere along the way, Patricia dies and rises over and over again hoping to appease a host of local and national deities whose favor she desires to win. The irony of both these kids is that one will succeed financially and socially more than the other, but neither can focus well. Pete, in a smoke-filled haze and its aftermath, can't bring things into focus, and Patricia can't sit still long enough to focus even if her goals can be clearly stated and achieved.

Attention deficit/hyperactivity disorder (ADHD), formerly called attention deficit disorder (ADD), has become part of the American adolescent experience regarding diagnosis and medication. Now, I'm not a doctor or a neuroscientist, but the issues of Pete and Patricia are at least loosely connected to how we deal culturally and individually with lack of attention. In a brief and informative article, Amanda Morin lists what she refers to as things kids with ADHD may not be able to do:

- Know when to focus on small details and when to focus on the bigger picture
- Filter out unimportant sights, sounds, or information
- Pay attention without getting distracted
- Hold a train of thought when interrupted
- Follow through on a task without needing to hear directions several times
- Concentrate on one activity at a time
- Follow spoken directions
- Process information quickly
- Keep up in conversation

Both of the student types formerly mentioned may have some of these traits without actually being formally diagnosed as ADHD. However, the cynicism of Pete and the socially acceptable neurosis of Patricia are part of larger cultural issues of distraction. Problems of filtering, prioritizing, and general singularity in conversation, direction, and attention are something we have not mastered despite significant technological and medical advances. It isn't hard to imagine a polytheistic world of sacrifices and festivals that would drive the neurotic to keep a frightful list, push the cynic to greater lows, and keep everyone else in an obedient herd. The singularity of the first commandment is a prioritizing that couldn't exist in Egypt unless perhaps you found yourself under a local deity and only had to keep track of the other gods in seasonal form or during significant festivals.

In another related article, titled "Ten Reasons Your Child Can't Focus That Aren't ADD," the following are listed: lack of practice, doesn't understand the material, isn't being challenged enough, is distracted by external stimuli, has a lack of motivation, has mismatched learning style, is not getting proper sleep or nutrition, has disorganization problems, has school anxiety, or has learning difficulties.[2]

So, since I'm not looking at this medically, I will admit that it does exist, and to look at our attention issues regarding the first commandment, I'll leave the debate over how to treat medical attention deficits to medical experts. The symptoms of what students struggle with do, however, fit into this ancient puzzle. For example, distraction, anxiety over focus, and various levels of paranoia or depression over performance and anxiety have striking parallels with the first commandment's contrast to the polytheistic pantheon of Egyptian worship. All the Egyptian gods were not equal, and it doesn't take a lot of research to find as to which deities were regional and which were national. The plagues preceding the Exodus give a solid context to the wording, "I am the Lord your God, who brought you out of Egypt, out of the land of slavery." Egypt was

---

2. "Ten reasons your child can't focus that aren't ADD." OxfordLearning.com. March 15, 2010.

far more powerful than ancient Israel and considerably wealthier. As a result, they did have slaves and quite a few of them. They also had gods for every natural need and a detailed belief system for life after death. Each of the plagues clashed with the gods the Egyptians worshipped and offered sacrifices to for life and fertility. In the ancient world, life and fertility covered just about all issues. So, it's not an accident that so many of the gods were connected to the Nile since that's what the Egyptians depended on. However, it is striking that despite the needs of Egypt fitting into two categories, they still had multiple gods in each category. And even though most teenagers and adults would look at Egyptian mythology in the way we use the word "myth," (i.e., a story that is interesting and superstitious), it is telling that so many of our "needs" fit into just a few categories. So many overachieving students become driven adults who need, among other things, bigger houses, more significant bank accounts, more clothes, and so on. Our academic résumés need to be diverse and, as adults, so do our financial portfolios. The idea of focusing on one thing is still connected to the understanding of excellence but is a considerable risk, as students and adults are taught not to put all their eggs in one basket, and by eggs, we mean hopes. So, the reality of divided attention pulls us to make sacrifices to various divine vending machines. Our children must be athletic; artistic; academic; and of course, have all the expected résumé builders, including volunteer work, which will give them the life they want. This is a very high, very stretched view of success. Our view of success is undoubtedly material, but it is also very diverse in a polytheistic way that involves many constant sacrifices. Of course, we usually present the finished product to others as our trophies, but undoubtedly, we are owned by what we own and by what we aspire to. Indeed, our dependency on others ideas in raising children and educating them is not free, either financially or psychologically, much less spiritually. So, it's little wonder that Americans spend an exorbitant amount of money on medication that, they expect, will help their children to focus better. Lawrence Diller, in a 2001 interview for PBS, answers concerning the lawsuit's alleged conspiracy:

> There's a suit going on right now in three states. It alleges that the major pharmaceutical company that makes Ritalin, the Novartis Company, along with the American Psychiatric Association, the leading representatives of organized medicine in the ADHD movement, and the self-help group CHADD have conspired to dupe the American public into believing that there's such a thing as ADHD and then thrust upon innocent children a potentially dangerous drug.
>
> The suit alleges that there's a conspiracy. Now, there may be some legal definition that meets the conspiracy angle. But I don't believe that there's any conspiracy at all. We have what I call the "invisible hand" of Adam Smith at work. Adam Smith, as you know, wrote the fundamental textbook on capitalism. And we have market forces at major play here, getting people to think a certain way about medications, and then operating on the doctors and the patients to get them to take them first—often at the expense of other interventions that work.

In the same article, Peter Breggin argues that children are the next big market:

> There are many, many reasons why we're giving more and more psychiatric drugs to children. Probably the most important reason is simple marketing. The drug companies, like the tobacco industry, like the alcohol industry, are highly competitive and are always searching out new markets. The adult market has been saturated for antidepressant drugs. How many millions and millions of people can take Prozac and Zoloft and all the other drugs? We have more adults taking antidepressants than the National Institute of Mental Health estimates there are depressed people in the United States. The market is saturated, so the pressures move automatically to other markets. And the biggest next market is children. So, you have drug company representatives; you have drug company-sponsored conferences examining this issue or encouraging this issue of marketing to children.[3]

---

3. Diller, Lawrence. Frontline.com. 2001.

Several other experts are interviewed, and it is fascinating but not surprising to see that Ritalin and Prozac have been marketed to children, bringing us full circle to Pete and his cynicism and Patricia and her driven neurosis. These two students and their struggles bring us back to the commandment, which pushes God to the front of the line and demands priority over all other gods. It also claims freedom with no immediate demand for sacrifice. Yes, that comes later, but the direct claim, the claim of mastery, is the source of liberty. Interestingly, the worship of this one God does not promise wealth and is not connected to any drug whatsoever. The ancient Egyptians, Mayans, South East Asians, and Indians all incorporated stimulants and hallucinogens into their belief systems. Certainly, medication is, along with self-help and psychology, the highest most likely form of what we could call worship in our society.

In fact, in a 2010 article, titled "Adderall May Not Make You Smarter, but It Makes You think You Are," Meredith Melnik points out that college students who are not ADHD use Adderall and Ritalin to get ahead. A study done by the University of Pennsylvania found that the only difference between students who took Adderall and a placebo was that those on Adderall felt they were more productive. As for the value of feeling more productive, excerpts from the writing samples of two students were included in the article by Molly Young.

Writing for *N+1*, Young noted, "Of course, I could have studied in college without Adderall, just like I did in high school—I just couldn't have studied with such ecstasy." Then again, ecstasy doesn't necessarily mean creativity, which is another marker of cognitive performance and one that's hard to pin down in a scientific study.[4]

"Though I could put more words to the page per hour on Adderall, I had a nagging suspicion that I was thinking with blinders on," wrote Slate's Joshua Foer in 2005.[5]

---

4. Melnick, Meredith. "Adderall may not make you smarter, but it makes you think you are." *Time Magazine*. December 21, 2010.

5. Foer, Joshua. "Ritalin vs adderall vs concerta: Which ADHD drug poses

Contrast our culture's use of drugs, tied to extremely diverse and probably unrealistic expectations, with the first commandment's claim and stipulation: "You were slaves I freed; you owe me your freedom instead of all these other gods."

---

the most risk for abuse." Ashewoodrecovery.com.

Chapter Two

God Makers

You shall not make for yourself an image in the form of anything in heaven above or on the earth beneath or in the waters below. You shall not bow down to them or worship them; for I, the Lord your God, am a jealous God, punishing the children for the sin of the parents to the third and fourth generation of those who hate me, but showing love to a thousand generations of those who love me and keep my commandments.

—EXOD. 20:4–6

IN 1989, Andre Agassi, rising tennis star and Hollywood heartthrob, filmed a commercial with the catchphrase "Image Is Everything." Steve Tignor, in a 2015 *Tennis.com* article, describes Agassi's initial asking about the line and then shrugging it off as part of the commercial. The phrase stuck, and not only was it recognizable but it also became a personal mantra as his fans chanted it to him as his on-court persona became louder, flashier, and more flamboyant. Tignor describes Agassi's use of a wig for a long time after he realized that his less than image-worthy baldness was becoming more prominent. In his autobiography, *Open*, Agassi describes the pressure of upholding an image of being the bad boy of tennis and his disillusionment even after reaching the number-one ranking. This disillusionment reached new lows with a temporary hatred of the game itself and experimentation with drugs. Agassi's story isn't completely hopeless, but it shows the pressures of being a public image. Tignor describes him as the closing of a decade of greed.[1] In today's world, the camera and image would seem to be the universal language. Images are the language of advertising, and media travels at the speed of the Internet. It would seem that our current age is the most image driven yet. Between character limits on Twitter, labeled memes, and the rise of Snapchat and Instagram, it isn't hard to see how we use words less and less in a world dominated by pictures. Also, our images are more easily doctored than ever before. "Doctored" is the right word because, from the early days of airbrushing and clumsy photoshopped pictures to today's camera phones that allow almost anyone to edit their pictures to a social media–deified state, we are a people of the image. The second commandment's prohibition against graven images seems either archaic or monstrously closed-minded. In 2001, Mullah Omar, the leader of the Taliban in Afghanistan, blew up ancient Buddha statues carved in the side of the mountains. The Western world recoiled at such demolition of history, statues that were constructed around 507 CE. Surely, that sort of prohibition doesn't belong in our modern world and can only lead to intolerance and destruction. Still, the prohibition is clear, to not make images resembling anything in the heaven (the sky), the earth, or the sea as an object of worship. So, worship, not artistic expression, is the issue. That brings up the question, what is worship? The immediate answer, given by many of my students and, frankly, most adults is some vague mention of what people do in churches. They may even add religious words like "praise." They will add such words without defining them either, which muddies up the issue for those unfamiliar with the religious language and also demonstrates their lack of understanding of the terms they use in their communities. It might be easy to point out the way we idolize celebrities, and we surely do, but why the need to make an

---

1. Tignor, Steve. 1989: "Image is Everything" Tennis.com. August 30, 2015

idol in the first place? Why move so quickly from admiration to something that seems like worship? There's something in human nature that wants to put the truly important in visible, tangible terms. This may not be idol worship, but it isn't very far away when we seek to control and quantify things that are beyond us. The average teenage pop song has something to do with love, which is expressed on the level of feelings. Beyond that, the lyrics usually take on life and death at some level. The lyrics of the average pop song would seem drastic were it not for the catchy tune and rhythmical beat. The expressions of adolescence are extreme and immediate, and the songs pander to these expressions on a dangerous and immediate level, not unlike some pagan sacrifice. Of course, my analogy might seem extreme, but the reaction of despair is nothing short of a crisis of religious intensity. A new study by Vanderbilt University found that between 2008 and 2015, the number of school-age children hospitalized for suicidal thoughts and actions had doubled.[2] This level of intensity matches the ancient world's religious fervor, and the gods that teens offer themselves to are quite similar to those of ancient Egyptian fame. Perhaps adolescents are more obvious, but it is clear that Western society worships the material and the emotional. Our houses, cars, and fashion are marketed unceasingly, and our desire for eternal youth is easily spotted in the continuous onslaught of beauty, youthfulness, and sexual prowess products. A woman's wrinkles can paradoxically cause her to spiral into depression unless the right anti wrinkle cream is used. Similarly, the right supplement is not only expected to build muscle in an aging man but also land him a beautiful and much younger woman. Teenagers are bombarded with visual messages that the right clothes, shoes, and acne medicine will give them confidence and romance. None of these messages are nearly as dangerous when they are only word oriented. The question "Don't you want to look and feel younger?" is not as alluring without a before and after picture. So, the teenager who sinks into an eating disorder because she isn't the measurements

---

2. Korte, Laura. "Youth suicide rates are rising, school and internet may be to blame." *Cincinnati Enquirer.* May 30, 2017.

she sees in an advertisement is driven by an image, and perhaps even an image that doesn't exist (especially if it is online).

Our views of wealth are also image driven. Who hasn't seen images of beautiful people partying with no regard for expense? The places, cars, meals, and fashion on display are taken to be the measure of wealth. In reality, people other than celebrities may have no idea of what that kind of wealth truly looks like or feels like. Does all the money come from entertainment? Do all rich people look much younger than they are? Are all wealthy people happy? The answer to these questions may be both complicated and simple at the same time, but if we are honest, we can very well see that our ideas of wealth and pleasure come from the images we are fed. This past year's revelations from the Me Too movement uncovered tales of shocking abuse of women and men in the world of entertainment. For an average person, the stories of assault and harassment border on the ridiculous in the obviousness of their evil. Could it be that because we have given image makers the place of idol makers, we don't want to hear that what the world worships is both dangerous and vulgar? In ancient Egypt, ceremonies involved a great deal of costume and makeup. Their gods were often people with animal heads, and expressions of fertility were both overtly sexual and animal. Before we dismiss ancient paganism as superstitious and not as advanced or evolved as we are today, it would help to see how sexualized our images are. The graven image prohibition is most effective not as a codified don't-do-this rule but as a principle drawn from the narrative. So are the things we choose to worship a mirror to what those things ask or expect of us? If the Egyptians—the most advanced and wealthiest people of their time—spent so much time worshipping things they thought would give them wealth, sexual prowess, and power, how much of it worked to their expectations? After all, they were the wealthiest and most powerful people of their time. So it must have worked, right? That's the clincher for the American adolescent and most adults: does it work? It very well may. If you want to look younger, the marketed diet, exercise, and clothes may make you look younger. If you want to find a beautiful partner, the self-help and dating book and seminar might work. If you want to be famous, you may need to break some rules. If, by chance, you don't have immediate consequences along the way, you may achieve a level of status that gives you at least some exceptionality regarding not getting the consequences normal people get. How many times have you turned on the news or seen the cover of a magazine showing a celebrity wrapping their car around a tree or showing up to work drunk or high and not losing their job? Even recovery from or apology for such acts gains status, and we would have to admit—if we were to ever take the time to think it through—that our idea of confession and recovery comes more from images than words or actions. The prohibition against sacred images forces us to resort to words. Words are both more descriptive and more imaginative, but they don't grab our immediate attention the way images do. Many times, when I teach poetry, I will use song lyrics to introduce students to the various terms and approaches of writing and understanding poems. There are some songs whose lyrics can be called poetic, but it is also fun to strip away the dance tracks and backbeats and expose bad lyrics for the trite, hyperbolic messes that they are. However, when words are not the focus, there is a lack of connection between reality and understanding. The fashion industry is a prime example of images we have accepted as fashionable—bizarre dresses that in reality cannot be worn by almost anyone, including the models who wear them and that too only for the tiniest fraction of time. On the other hand, words can point to transcendence that goes beyond the image or image bearer. The poet Byron, no friend to any sort of relational integrity, still penned these words:

> She walks in beauty, like the night
> Of cloudless climes and starry skies;
> And all that's best of dark and bright
> Meet in her aspect and her eyes:
> Thus mellowed to that tender light
> Which heaven to gaudy day denies.

One shade the more, one ray the less,
Had half impaired the nameless grace
Which waves in every raven tress,
Or softly lightens o'er her face;
Where thoughts serenely sweet express
How pure, how dear their dwelling place.

And on that cheek, and o'er that brow,
So soft, so calm, yet eloquent,
The smiles that win, the tints that glow,
But tell of days in goodness spent,
A mind at peace with all below,
A heart whose love is innocent![3]

Even students who don't like poetry are often struck by both the passion and principle of the lines. Contrast that with the lyrics of many rap songs. Naomi Wilson writes of a culture where rape is accepted as part of a genre. She lists lyrics which refer to slapping and stomping on victims and referring to women as part of a collection. Wilson's article is not timid in listing graphic acts, and finally admits some degree of complicity when she states "Am I condoning rap culture because I dance to a Future or DMX song in the shower? Maybe. Throughout the '90's and still today, hip-hop music promotes physical abuse towards women, uses derogatory terms towards women and encourages the practice of raping women."[4]

The contrast is obvious. The innocence of Byron's subject is worth admiring and worth protecting while object in the rap lyrics is purely prey or the decorative aspect of a violent fantasy. I think I could find examples of lyrics that matched Byron's tone and, perhaps at least after a significant search, his artistry and content (though I doubt it). However, the fact that the rappers mentioned in Wilson's article are quite successful, and multi-platinum

3. Gordon, George (Lord Byron). "She Walks in Beauty." Poems.org
4. Wilson, Naomi. "How men in hip-hop perpetuate mistreatment of women." Media Milwaukee December 24, 2017.

recording star Jay Z performed at President Obama's inauguration says something about what we excuse when the image and beat are to our liking. There may be layers to these men that I don't know. I assume that since I don't know them. The point still stands that many of, in fact most of, their lyrics are as openly misogynist and predatory as the ones mentioned in the previous article. The current images of them as a concerned family men may have some truth. But an examination of the words of these songs reveals that they are at tremendous odds with their art. Therein lies the key to understanding why, when we as humans make idols, they are so much more likely to be imaged.

For years, high-school juniors were all required to read F. Scott Fitzgerald's *The Great Gatsby*. The principal plot line of Fitzgerald's novel is the character Jay Gatsby's obsession with a lost love of his, Daisy Buchanan. Daisy is perfect in his memory, and he sets out to win her over even though she has already married another man. Gatsby, though he was beneath Daisy's social class, manages through illegitimate means to amass a tremendous amount of wealth. He builds an enormous house across the lake from where daisy lives and throws elaborate parties in the hopes that such spectacles will eventually attract her attention and give him the chance to win her over and show her his love. Each night he stares across the lake at the green light in front of Daisy's mansion. Throughout our general class discussions, my students will pick up the importance of the green light as a motif. I'm not sure if they identify it as important because of its repeated color mention or because it is mentioned in SparkNotes. In either case, it does matter, and although it symbolizes Gatsby's obsession, only the most insightful students usually pick up the significance of the color green. Once I bring up the color green, mostly everyone makes connections to money and nature. However, eventually, we come around to the point that the light is entirely artificial and that its color, green, although a natural color, is entirely man-made here. So, with Gatsby's obsession, the reality of what he calls love and commitment is entirely artificial. In the end, Daisy, despite her unfaithful husband's boorish nature, doesn't leave her marriage to start over with Gatsby. Gatsby himself takes the blame for Daisy running over Tom's mistress with Gatsby's car. Perhaps the most telling scene in the book occurs before the climax, when George Wilson, Myrtle's husband, has confronted his wife despite not knowing how she is cheating or who her lover is.

> "I spoke to her," he muttered, after a long silence. "I told her she might fool me, but she couldn't fool God. I took her to the window—" With an effort, he got up and walked to the rear window and leaned with his face pressed against it, "—and I said 'God knows what you've been doing, everything you've been doing. You may fool me, but you can't fool God!'"
> Standing behind him Michaelis saw with a shock that he was looking at the eyes of Dr. T. J. Eckleburg, which had just emerged pale and enormous from the dissolving night.
> "God sees everything," repeated Wilson.
> "That's an advertisement," Michaelis assured him. Something made him turn away from the window and look back into the room. But Wilson stood there a long time, his face close to the window pane, nodding into the twilight. (8.72–105)

George Wilson, the only genuine character in the novel, has no connection to anything religious, by his own admission. He does, however, in his attempt at clarity, have an idea that God sees, even if his point of reference is a billboard for an optometrist. Fitzgerald gives the reader a sincere but naïve character in a slew of men and women who exist to gratify their pleasures. George Wilson is poorer than the other characters and, at best, is secondary to the plot. Still, the main characters, especially Gatsby and Nick, live in a world of infidelity and wealth. Jay Gatsby, the plot's focus, lives obsessed with one woman so much that he openly states that he can change the past: not only will he—at least he believes he can—win Daisy from her husband but he will also change the things that transpired that caused her to marry her current husband, and he will do this by winning her over. In the end, boorish, rich, old Tom Buchanan offers too much status for Daisy to risk leaving him. Tom plays his cards perfectly, arrogantly confronting Gatsby and exposing Gatsby's bootlegging wealth source. So even Gatsby's wealth isn't enough for him to rewrite history. With all the novel's exposé of the hollow nature of wealth and status, the narrator, Nick Caraway, still identifies Gatsby as better than the rest, the rest being those who are stuck in the vapid nature of wealth, infidelity, and status. In the closing of the novel Nick states:

> They're a rotten crowd . . . You're worth the whole damn bunch put together . . . And as I sat there brooding on the old, unknown world, I thought of Gatsby's wonder when he first picked out the green light at the end of Daisy's dock. He had come a long way to this blue lawn and his dream must have seemed so close that he could hardly fail to grasp it. He did not know that it was already behind him, somewhere back in that vast obscurity beyond the city, where the dark fields of the republic rolled on under the night.
> Gatsby believed in the green light, the orgiastic future that year by year recedes before us. It eluded us then, but that's no matter—tomorrow we will run faster, stretch out our arms farther . . . And one fine morning—
> So, we beat on, boats against the current, borne back ceaselessly into the past. (9.151–154)

In death, Gatsby becomes the American Dream regarding those who have not inherited wealth and had to strive for it. Nick canonizes him for his singular focus and uses the green light as the motif for a man who has a singularity of commitment in his striving amid a world of wealth where no one has to commit or work because everyone has been given the wealth and status they subsist on. His superiority over the other characters comes from his singular striving. Daisy cannot leave Tom because she cannot exist outside of the wealth her marriage gives her. Jordan Baker, Nick's onetime lover, cannot commit to him because her independence comes from her wealth as well. Nick, for a time, admires the many characters he fraternizes with because of their opulent lifestyle. In reality, the characters of the novel remain the same, callous because of their extreme privilege. They may live as masters, but spiritually and psychologically, they are slaves to their wealth. In the end, Nick leaves the Northeast and heads back West in a sort of secular exodus. Even in the cherished American Dream with only one religious reference in the whole novel, there is a parody of sorts with the surviving narrator leaving the slavery of Egypt to escape its wealth and the gods who demand him as a sacrifice for the pleasures of a luxurious life of excess. Gatsby may well be better because he had a singular focus, but the object of his worship was far too weak and shallow to give him any real redemption.[5]

One more novel stands out in my experience as demonstrating through its narrative the gutting reality of worshiping an image. Once a commonly read novel, Charles Dickens's *Great Expectations* is more likely to be collecting dust in some corner today. Still, despite its length, I have periodically used the original and adapted versions in classes from the ninth to the twelfth grade. Once again one man's obsession with a woman embodies the soul-numbing risk of worshiping an image. However, in the grossly unequal relationship between Pip, the protagonist, and Estella, the worshiped woman, the reader gets to see the nature of both the man who worships an image and the cruelty of the idol itself. Estella is an orphan raised by the extremely eccentric character Miss Havisham. Miss Havisham is a wealthy woman who upon being stood up at the altar spends her life raising a beautiful young girl, who in the words of the novel is to "wreak havoc on the male sex." Miss Havisham, as is to be expected, is extremely wealthy. It's much easier to produce an idol when you have the means to display it in a way that makes it attractive, even seductive. Pip being set up to look up to and fall in love with Estella is Miss Havisham's plan all along. However, her cruelty extends beyond her original intent when Pip is anonymously adopted by a benefactor who gives Pip a shot at a wealthy life. This, instead of giving Pip a chance to escape both poverty and Estella just plunges him more deeply into his obsession with a woman who both reacts and seduces him according to the pattern set up by her adopted mother. Along the way, Pip comes to realize how destructive his attraction to Estella is. His best friend warns

---

5. Fitzgerald, F. Scott. *The Great Gatsby*. Scribner 2018.

him of it, and eventually, even Estela tries to warn him, explaining that she herself is not capable of love. In the end, Pip chooses his obsession with winning Estella and the status he thinks he needs to accomplish this over his family who loves him. When his wealth comes to a tragic end, he is left with only those who love him, albeit damaged by his unrequited love. The novel's ending, which involves Miss Havisham's realization of what she has created, Estella's entrance into an abusive marriage, and Pip's loss of his wealth, is somewhat redemptive though. This is perhaps Dickens's genius in bringing together multiple plot lines but ending in realistic ambiguity. However, the tie to the second commandment remains in that Pip and Estella, who is eventually widowed from a violent husband, are not together. Their paths have brought them back together, but Pip still clings to his obsession with a person who is no longer abusive and projects onto Estella goddess-like expectations. The lesson of *Great Expectations,* which ties most closely to the Commandments, is that idols damage their makers and their worshipers; they fail to fulfill the worshiper and corrupt the worshiped. So, Miss Havisham's desire to save an orphan from the cruelties of the world ends up being a means of revenge that creates a monster. She cannot control a pattern that recreates the abusive behavior she had suffered at the hands of the man who had stood her up at the altar. Not as overtly vulgar as some rap lyrics but just as predatory, Estella becomes what Daryl Hall and John Oates called a man-eater. So graven images are the misuse of that which can be useful in their original purpose but become extremely dangerous once elevated to divine status. So, the Egyptian gods that mimicked natural patterns and animals themselves become controlling rituals that excuse slavery and, in the case of the Middle Kingdom of Egypt, may have even demanded human sacrifice.[6] Going back to the hallways of the average public school and perhaps even the boardrooms of major corporations, it isn't hard to see the suicidal impact of the gods we elevate in exchange

---

6. Gee, John, and Kerry Muhlestein. "An Egyptian context for the sacrifice of Abraham." Journal of the Book of Mormon and other Restoration Scripture 2011.

for the sacrifices we give to attain success. One final note needs to be addressed before moving to the third commandment. That is the issue of jealousy connected to the prohibition of making and having graven images. The modern and postmodern reader may struggle with the divine admission of being jealous. Isn't jealousy for insecure lovers and troubled relationships? First of all, the proportion of those who are rejected by a jealous God is telling. Those who face his punishment for disobedience are to the third and fourth generation while those who are rewarded for obedience are the children of the thousandth generation. There's no need to gloss over the difficulty of wrath and jealousy, but it is noteworthy that the blessing is for the future generations—that is, rewards are received that have not been earned. This does two things. It extends generosity well beyond those who have earned it and breaks the constant cycle of sacrifice assumed in the ancient world. The centuries spent in slavery are rewarded with millennia of freedom based on the commands. With Gatsby and Pip in mind, it also is quite possible that freedom isn't a this-for-that type of reward as much as it is a lifestyle of commitment that keeps people from following gods who would lead them glibly back into a life of slavery. There is no illusion that life might include pleasures but rather a warning that in the end, it is slavery, and there is no way out unless the Exodus includes leaving the place and the practices of the slave masters. The issue of jealousy and love has come up in my teaching of *Le Morte d'Arthur* and *Don Quixote*. It is tricky at first because it is tied up with some of the odder rituals of courtly love. However, when the class discussion turns to the rules of courtly love, the one that usually sparks interest and, in large part, agreement is that no true lover exists without the potential of jealousy. Most students readily agree that a person who feels no jealousy can't be in love with someone. What can be said for a lover who is cheated on but is also unfazed by the infidelity?[7] Pip upon finding out that Estella is marrying his brutish, snobbish archrival, Bentley Drummle, begs Estella not to marry the man. He even pleads with her to marry someone else even if it isn't Pip himself. He does this because he

---

7. Mallory, Thomas. *Le Morte d'Arthur*; Cervantes, Miguel. *Don Quixote*.

knows Estella will just be a status symbol for Drummle—whose wealthy status causes him to think that he is entitled to a trophy wife—to possess. Tom, Daisy's boorish husband, is confident that Daisy won't leave him because of the status he provides. After the confrontation, Tom allows Daisy to drive home with Gatsby because he knows he has won. His jealousy does not come from love but rather from a sense of triumph over his rival. Daisy will remain his possession because of the status she risks in leaving Tom. The God of the Exodus does not offer wealth or status as rewards for those who keep his commandments but rather offers the path of freedom, which is the path away from slavery and the gods of the slave masters

Chapter Three

What Did You Say?

> You shall not misuse the name of the Lord your God,
> for the Lord will not hold anyone guiltless who misuses his name.
>
> —EXOD. 20:7

THE third commandment is often interpreted as being a sort of profanity, whose punishment would be a divine getting your mouth washed out with soap. The problem with this interpretation is the translation and the context. An oath in the ancient world was not profanity but a binding agreement. Oral tradition meant oral contracts, and as a result, the breaking of an oath was legally punishable. However, that still isn't the original interpretation of taking the Lord's name in vain. In reality, this commandment was for people who had already accepted the claims of the ancient Hebrew God. In other words, it isn't the first commandment for reasons of order. You have to place this God above all others, not substitute him with graven images and, as a result, not take his name lightly. So, this would include things like false prophecy or ordinary usage. The ancient Hebrews and modern orthodox Jews will leave the "*o*" out of the written spelling of the word "God."[1] And

---

1. Orthodox Orthograph: Why No "O" in God. beliefnet.com.

unlike American evangelicals, the term "Lord" was not a constant to their vocabulary; it was a substitutionary word for one of the actual names of God. So, in an ancient world of gods, it is easy to see how misrepresenting the nature of the one true God would be so serious. Once again, the nature of false prophecy ties into the order of the Commandments given. If the Hebrew God is the God of freedom and freedom is not tied to multiple sacrifices to multiple gods with the need to appease them to obtain their favor, then it is easier to see this command's connection to present-day Americans. Aside from "Don't be disrespectful" or "Don't use one more swear word," let's just start with the obvious. All of human history is littered with empires claiming the blessings of their gods in conquering others. Sam Harris in his *Letters to a Christian Nation* offers this rebuke:

> Christians have abused, oppressed, enslaved, insulted, tormented, tortured, and killed people in the name of God for centuries, by a theologically defensible reading of the Bible.[2]

Now Harris marks Christianity specifically and religion, in general, but since his critique mentions the use of Christianity to abuse others, it helps to understand the third commandment. I'm pretty sure Harris might not be thrilled with me using his quote to explain the Commandments, but I'll assume he is a reasonable conversationalist. Plus, he is also not present with me as I write this. For the sake of narrowing the application, I'll just stick to the United States. Early in US history, Western expansion was supported through a doctrine known as Manifest Destiny, which substituted the United States into Old Testament passages about the promised land. In establishing the KKK, postwar Southerners claimed Christianity even as they espoused anti-Semitism. So, what does this have to do with the third commandment? Simply put, it speaks against exercising unauthorized and unjustified power over another in the name of the divine. It isn't just an excuse

---

2. Harris, Sam. *Letters to A Christian Nation.* First Vintage Books Edition, January 2008.

for bad behavior because one doesn't need the divine to rationalize. However, large-scale rationalization requires a larger object of focus for excusing such actions. At this point, it would seem like I'm selling the farm to the Harris argument. I'm assuming the Egyptian nature of human worship, at least the ancient Egyptian variety—a pantheon of gods for wealth and pleasure or a singular excuse for power. Both cases require slavery, and the Commandments are for the free. So, since the Commandments, starting with the first, are for the free but don't promise wealth or pleasure, the misuse of the name of God is just one more sign of slavery. However, it isn't as simple a case-closed proposition as it sounds. In the humorously titled book *Will Jesus Buy Me a Double-Wide: Because I Need More Room for My Plasma TV*, author Karen Spears Zacharias makes the following claim:

> We Americans want to believe that God loves us best of all and that all of our nation's riches are the result of our faithfulness to God . . . Entitlement theology may very well be the bastard-child born from the mating of Calvinism's strong work ethic with Capitalism's get-all-the-goods-you-can mentality.[3]

This claim alone backs up the first three commandments with a particular focus on the third. If we need to be above others and don't want to claim divinity, then claiming the divine right is the next best thing. Consider Russell Moore's blog post "What a Stupid Bumper Sticker Can Tell Us about American Christianity." In this post, author Russell Moore points out a recent bumper sticker he read that states, "If Jesus had had a gun, he'd be alive today." Moore readily points out the awkward irony of someone who probably goes to church and marries their politics to a gun control argument that assumes that Jesus is dead.[4] To Sam Harris, this makes no difference, but to someone who supposedly believes in the resurrection, this is beyond ironic, and for what purpose? To argue

---

3. Zacharias, Karen Spears. "Will Jesus buy me a double wide? Cause I need more room for my plasma TV." Zondervan 2010.

4. Moore, Russell. "What a stupid bumper sticker can tell us about American Christianity." Russelmoore.com. December 11, 2017

for gun control. In this case, the drivers who plastered the sticker on the back of their cars were spreading around a political view using religious language, a violation of the third commandment. Better yet, consider the past presidential election cycle where supporters of Donald Trump wore T-shirts emblazoned with "Thank You Jesus for President Trump." And what about the Osteens, Joel and Victoria, whose prosperity gospel message has made them millions. Her most famous quote about worship is stated clearly:

> When we obey God; we're not doing it for God; we're doing it for ourselves. Do good for yourself. Do it because God wants you to be happy. When you come to church when you worship Him, you're not doing it for God, really—you're doing it for yourself, because that's what makes God happy. Amen?[5]

So, much like the pantheon of ancient deities you sacrificed to, hoping to appease and get something back from, the Osteens promise health and wealth. They, of course, live a life of luxury that backs up their claims to believe as they do and pay at the door. The problem is that, as Spears Zacharias points out, many of those who buy this pay-to-play theology are those who are in the worst condition financially. In a 2016 article in *CNN*'s Business section, Ahiza Garcia points out the place of the poor in playing the lottery. Multiple studies in states such as Texas, Connecticut, South Carolina, and Minnesota have shown that the majority of people who play instant lotto games have below-average incomes.[6]

The reason? "Winning $5,000 on an instant game is a huge amount of money if you're struggling financially—it can be life changing for someone just trying to get by," said Victor Matheson, an economics professor at the College of the Holy Cross.

Lotteries are sometimes criticized as a "de facto tax on the poor," according to Matheson. "The poor spend a much higher

---

5. https://www.brainyquote.com/lists/authors/top_10_victoria_osteen_quotes.

6. Garcia, Ahiza. CNNBusiness.com. January 12, 2016

percentage of their overall income on lotteries than the rich, and they can afford it less," he said.[7]

So since getting rich is the American Dream, the lottery is like a Gatsby story without the illegal activity. The players offer the sacrifice of their meager incomes and hope for blessings.

People like the Osteens just attach religious language to their works, but even a cursory look at their statements shows that the language isn't even that religious. The ancient Egyptians were perhaps a bit more honest, but all that still doesn't dispute the third commandment, which is less of a wash out of your potty mouth and more a warning that you are about to get fleeced, and it is still not what the first commandment called freedom. The American school hallways have T-shirts with such visible slogans as "Money over Everything" and various other aspiring-rich mottos. Even a teacher I worked with, who otherwise was quite respectable, had a poster labeled "Justification for higher learning" that had a large mansion with $100,000 cars in its large, winding driveway. So the final adolescent example of why we can't seem to keep the third commandment might well be the high-school youth-group kids who are so often ardently against welfare and segregated in their groups. Either they are being taught such categories or more likely the preaching of the third commandment is limited in their churches to not saying things like OMG.

---

7. Isidore, Chris. "We spend billions on lottery tickets. Here's where all that money goes." @CNNMoney. August 24, 2017 (4:44 p.m. ET).

Chapter Four

Working Ourselves to Death

Remember the Sabbath day by keeping it holy. Six days you shall labor and do all your work, but the seventh day is a sabbath to the Lord your God. On it you shall not do any work, neither you, nor your son or daughter, nor your male or female servant, nor your animals, nor any foreigner residing in your towns. For in six days, the Lord made the heavens and the earth, the sea, and all that is in them, but he rested on the seventh day. Therefore, the Lord blessed the Sabbath day and made it holy.

—EXOD. 20:8-11

IN 1981, the band Loverboy released a song titled "Everybody's Working for the Weekend." It was catchy, not too deep, and standard fare for what produced a hit then and may still show up on an eighties lunch radio show or some sort of a throwback party. Still, the sentiment is spot on for American culture, in that we work to play. Or at least that's what we say. Another cliché thrown around is "Work hard, play harder," but that may not entirely be it either. Abigail Hess of *CNBC News* reports that Americans take fewer vacation days than their counterparts in other industrialized nations. Hess points out that according to a study from the U.S. Travel Association's "Project Time Off," 52 percent of Americans didn't even use all of their vacation days in 2017.

> Americans used to understand the importance of getting away from the office. From 1976 to 2000, the average working American took off more than 20 days a year. Starting in 2000, workers have been taking fewer days off. In 2015, American worked took an average of just 16 days off.

The article goes on to point out that in countries like Austria and France, governments require that workers are given paid time off. Austrians enjoy thirteen paid public holidays and twenty-five days of paid annual leave.[1] The *Boston Globe* reports that the United States is one of just thirteen countries in the world that does not guarantee paid time off.

"The United States is the only advanced economy in the world that does not guarantee its workers paid vacation days and paid holidays," says John Schmitt, vice president of the Economic Policy Institute, in a report for the Center for Economic and Policy Research.[2]

The economics of this are for a broader debate, but clearly, our clichés don't match up with our practice. If we couple this with our marketing push for technology that is supposed to give us more productivity and free time, the gap between reality and merchandising is getting bigger. John Steinbeck's classic American novel was published in 1937 but still speaks clearly to the hopelessness of never-ending work. The two main characters, George and Lennie, travel around together working at ranches and making enough to get by without any hope of actually settling down and owning anything of their own. The book builds its simple plot to a climax as George and Lennie go in with Candy, an old ranch hand who agrees to give them his life's meager savings and disability payment for a chance to buy a place of their own. The hope in the three

---

1. Hess, Abigail. *CNBC News.* 2017a.
2. Hess, Abigail. *CNBC News.* 2017b.

laborers is shattered when Lennie, the gentle giant and mentally handicapped man, accidentally kills the boss's son's wife. George is essentially euthanizing his unsuspecting friend, and Candy realizes that they aren't going to get a place and that he won't live out his final years with any type of independence or dignity. To understand Candy's despair, it's necessary to backtrack to an evening in the novel where Candy gets cornered by Carlson and is talked into letting him shoot his dog. Carlson argues over and over that Candy's dog is no good anymore, including to himself. Carlson gets Slim to give Candy one of his puppies in exchange for letting him shoot Candy's old dog. Not surprisingly, Candy's dog is unnamed. Later Candy tells George that he hopes that when he is no longer of use that someone will shoot him and that he should have shot the dog himself. This particularly hopeless view of a life of continuous work is extremely relevant to a society where work is supposed to be a means to an end that can never be reached. Dreams and advancement exist for those who can afford them, and those who can afford them could do so before they had to work. So, work is inevitable and has no higher purpose, and play is whatever gives relief from endless, pointless work. Thus, the laborers in *Of Mice and Men* go out on the weekends to spend what little money they have on alcohol or prostitutes, numbing the hopelessness and "getting it out of their system," as George refers to it.[3]

So, what does this have to do with the observance of the Sabbath? The Sabbath was a mandated day of rest. It was a sacred way to refocus and refuel. The ancient Hebrews were to rest regularly and not work endlessly. People, animals, and the land were all to rest. It was a divine mandate and its observance was meant to acknowledging that God was not a cruel landowner. Contrast this with slavery in Egypt. Slaves work endlessly, have little reward, and no incentive. In fact, in Exodus 5, Pharaoh, irritated by Moses, demands that the ancient Hebrews find and gather their own straw for brickmaking but keep the quota for production the same. This sort of unreasonable expectation with no accountability for the one in charge mirrors the hopelessness of the American laborers

3. Steinbeck, John. *Of Mice and Men*. Penguin Books 1965.

in *Of Mice and Men*. People who work with purpose but do not work endlessly are, Biblically speaking, free people.

Jay Gatsby answers work calls at his parties, George and Lennie never get a place of their own, and the American worker takes fewer days of vacation each year than they did thirty years ago. The fourth commandment has some value we don't espouse. The American high-school hallway is full of students who will graduate, just barely, and head out into a world of work with little preparation. Many times, because of a lack of focus, they will enter a world where one job will not be enough to cover necessities. Add a child or health issues, and employment will become truly stressful with no end in sight. So, with the high risk, how does the average student respond? Quite honestly, without much effort. Many high-school students coast through school either naïvely assuming they will be fine or nihilistically assuming that it was never going to be good anyway and so there was no use in trying. The second option is even more disturbing considering the opportunities available. Too many students accept hopelessness without having tried in the first place. The inevitable becomes a self-fulfilling prophecy.

On top of that is the use of technology. Technology for many teenagers is a way to tune out the world or perhaps just as much a way to tune into a more attractive world. A very bright student once told me that she watches videos on her phone because they are more interesting than a lot of things around her. Her answer is not unusual and didn't get in the way of her being a high-achieving student. But what about the students who aren't high achievers? Can they afford the distraction? And unlike the student mentioned, what about those who have little support at home? Many, and perhaps most, of the students I just described are not doing well academically or behaviorally. Many will say the system doesn't work for them. The system may have holes in it, or they may be facing severe disparities before they even walk in the door, but they are not doing anything that looks remotely hopeful. The language of such students is the language of hopelessness. A shoulder shrug or a look away is quite common for those who are coasting through. The irony of this is that those who begin with less and coast are those who will exit the school hallways with even more challenges and fewer possibilities. The videos they download, the music they are attached to, and the social media conspiracies espoused are no more real to them than the gods of Egypt, but they will hold on to hopelessness more than hope. The genius of the Sabbath was that it assumed meaningful work and mandated rest. The rest was not a result of wealth or privilege but was something divinely given for health, both physical and spiritual.

The ancient Hebrews had among them those wealthy and the poor, but no one was denied regular rest because it was part of work. You didn't have to assume that rest was far off or never coming. George and Lennie fall back on the distractions of cat houses and alcohol because of the endless hard work. The American teenager with their phone as an endless distraction is numbed from developing a work ethic, which might seem irrelevant, considering a lifetime of work ahead of them. However, unlike George and Lennie, the jobs the earbud students may get stuck in might not require the most significant effort and may mean years of more numbing technology. For the free, hard work has meaning, and rest is part of the package. For the numb, the Sabbath is meaningless because hopelessness needs no work ethic and technology self-medicates whatever pain goes with the slothfulness of a mundane existence of continuous employment.

Chapter Five

Mom, Dad and the You, You Can't See

Honor your father and your mother, so that you may live long in the land the Lord your God is giving you.

—EXOD. 20:12

MARK Twain quipped about his father, "When I was a boy of fourteen, my father was so ignorant I could hardly stand to have the old man around. But when I got to be twenty-one, I was astonished at how much he had learned in seven years." More brutally stated recently is David Hogg of March for Our Lives. He doesn't feel like he's the one who should be calling for this. "I shouldn't have to! I'm 17," he said, but he and his classmates feel that adults—both voters and policymakers—have failed them. "When your old-ass parent is like, 'I don't know how to send an iMessage,' and you're just like, 'Give me the f*cking phone and let me handle it.' Sadly, that's what we have to do with our government; our parents don't know how to use a f*cking democracy, so we have to."[1] Twain's humor softens the blow, but both are examples of

---

1. Miller, Lisa. *David Hogg, After Parkland. New York Magazine.* August 19, 2018.

the natural but painful process of growing up and individuating. Hogg's anger is the more specific response, but in a world where things aren't right, part of growing up is learning to care for and question what your parents cared for or did. There is also the question of how to or whether to honor parents who were damaging or even abusive, but more on that later. Psychologists refer to the process of becoming an individual independent of a community as individuating. I suppose the debate over how independent we are from our community could go on for a very long time, but it seems obvious enough to say that growing up and becoming independent is sometimes painful, and even functional families experience tension when a bird leaves the nest. In many cultures around the world, moving away and defining yourself outside your family is not as cherished a stage as we have made it in the United States. However, the process usually requires some distance even if that distance is just emotional or mental. Aside from living their dreams, most adolescents want to not end up like their parents or at least avoid the negative aspects of their parents' character. If a young girl wants to move out and move in with the love of her life, she doesn't want to hear from her divorced mom that he isn't such a good guy. It may be that mom's bad experiences give her an insight as to how the young stud is quite manipulative, but the daughter probably has disqualified her mom from commenting by pointing out that her life will be different from her mom who is stuck being single and couldn't make a marriage work. Mom may even counter that she knows how her daughter feels but that her former husband or the daughter's father pulled the wool over her eyes the way the young boyfriend is doing. This, of course, will probably go over horribly since tied up in the young love is also the tension of the lost dad, who isn't around to get mad at, so all anger will be focused on the one person who stayed, Mom. If this seems ironic, it may still ring true since the old cliché is often forceful in that we always hurt the ones we love. I've also heard it said that daughters usually marry men like their fathers and that is why mothers cry at weddings. I'm not sure if this is true, but just as our genetics usually turn us into something strikingly like our parents, our patterns of family are often, if not directly addressed, almost always directly repeated. So, children of divorced parents are more likely to get divorced, and tragically children who grow up in an abusive, violent home are more likely to become abusive or violent themselves.

Once again *Great Expectations* is both instructive and illustrative. Pip's adopted father, Joe Gargery, is beyond what anyone could call henpecked. His wife, the unnamed Mrs. Jo, is unapologetically and chronically abusive, insulting him, even hitting him, and forcing him to submit to her as if he were a naughty child. In one illuminating passage, Jo explains to Pip why his marriage is the way it is.

> And last of all, Pip—and this I want to say very serious to you, old chap—I see so much in my poor mother, of a woman drudging and slaving and breaking her honest hart and never getting no peace in her mortal days, that I'm dead afeerd of going wrong in the way of not doing what's right by a woman, and I'd fur rather of the two go wrong the t'other way, and be a little ill-conwenienced myself. I wish it was only me that got put out, Pip; I wish there weren't no Tickler for you, old chap; I wish I could take it all on myself; but this is the up-and-down-and-straight on it, Pip, and I hope you'll overlook shortcomings.[2]

Jo, in his fear of being an abusive man like his father, has allowed himself and Pip to be abused by his wife. Psychologically, Jo is his mother's son and, as a result, has married a woman just like his father. More than once Jo stands up for his house and his wife. He is not a man to be bullied and is imposing physically, but within his home, he is nonetheless a battered wife. Pip, in his haste to leave home and win Estella, never notices that Estella's vicious cruelty is remarkably like his sister's, who has raised him by continually berating and belittling him. Pip doesn't win over Estella but passes over the opportunity to be with Biddy, someone much

2. Dickens, Charles. *Great Expectations*. Glencoe/Mcgraw hill School pub. 2000.

more suitable to him. In the height of ironies, Biddy, after Mrs. Joe's death, marries Jo. Pip, in a confession to his closest friend Herbert, declares that he loves Estella. Hebert after trying to talk him out of this obsession mercifully stays his friend.

Jo doesn't grow old with a kind wife. The pattern repeated itself despite both characters attempting to escape their upbringing—Jo through not becoming the abuser and Pip through chasing after an abusive, manipulative woman. So, hindsight can make these things clear, but so many of them seem inevitable. In the inevitability, the fourth commandment allows for grace toward parents who may well be repeating patterns from their upbringing. It also provides for adolescents who want to take their upbringing seriously and perhaps somehow admit they might have developed the same blind spots. The second seems quite unlikely given the nature of adolescence. Mark Twain was funny and quite insightful in his take on his father. In either case, a gentler example is the character of Scout from Harper Lee's *To Kill a Mockingbird*. Scout and her brother Jem are initially frustrated with their father because he's grown older and can't play with them the way they would like. Throughout the novel, Atticus, Scout and Jem's father, takes on the enormous challenge of defending Tom Robinson, a black man who will stand trial before an all-white jury deep in the South. Though Scout is the narrator, it is Jem who realizes how strong his father is. Twenty-three chapters into a thirty-one chapter book, Jem is beginning to have conversations with Atticus about the law and inequalities. Jem explains to Scout that there are different kinds of people, and each group looks down on the group right below them. At this stage of the novel, mostly because of the brutal nature of the trial and false accusation of rape, Jem is beginning to see his father on adult terms. This then is a more straightforward example of honoring your father, because in this case, he is someone to look up to. It's no wonder then that when *Go Set a Watchman*, a never before released novel by Harper Lee, was published in 2015, many thought it was taking advantage of an elderly author who didn't fully understand her surroundings anymore or, worse, was written by someone else and released under the famed author's name who was suffering from dementia. *Go Set a Watchman* has the writing tone of *To Kill a Mockingbird*, and many who believe Harper Lee wrote it think of it as *Mockingbird's* rough and discarded draft. Whatever may be the truths in such a debate, the firestorm that came of it was Atticus. Atticus is not the pillar of integrity in *Watchman* that he is in *Mockingbird* but rather a man with some integrity who did his job but sees the state of the Southern "negro" as one of infancy and moral and intellectual childhood. Such people are not yet ready for integration. This Atticus seems to come from the same culture and period as his better-known avatar, but the reader will sympathize with Scout when she rails against his racism. She loves him and is loyal, but he does not inspire honor.[3] Therein lies the power of the fourth commandment. It is not raising parents as honorable by office or example but by drawing in the child and adolescent to a lesson that remains beyond them. All parents will fall short of their ideals, no matter how honorable they may be. Some parents are not even honorable in the ideas they espouse and fall short of. Some parents live up to their principles with evil consistency.

M. Scott Peck, in his book *People of the Lie*, writes of children whose parents could be called psychologically evil.

> It happens then that the children of evil parents enter adulthood with very significant psychiatric disturbances . . . It is doubtful that some can be wholly healed of their scars from having had to live in close quarters with evil without correctly naming the source of their problems.
>
> To come to terms with evil in one's parentage is perhaps the most difficult and painful psychological task a human being can be called on to face. Most fail, and so remain its victims. Those who fully succeed in developing the necessary searing vision are those who can name it.

In his book, Peck goes beyond psychological analysis and allows for the reality of the demonic and supernatural evil. This becomes problematic in his melding of psychology and theology that elevates free will to an immovable object. He goes so far as to say

3. Lee, Harper. *Go Set a Watchman*. Harper Collins 2015.

that God cannot move a person without their consent. This creates a tension with the fourth commandment in that free will becomes equal with God. Ironically, Sam Harris, one of the world's preeminent atheists, argues well against this view of free will and explains that what we call free will is often a created illusion because we spend so much of our time shaping our view of self—based on what we think others are thinking—that it has no basis in fact.

Nonetheless, the fourth commandment is a blunt barrier to Peck's strong examples of the adolescent view of free will and a hedge of protection for children of abusive parents. The fourth commandment states to honor your father and mother that your days may be long upon the earth. It is perhaps our modern obsession with fairness and free will that leaves us blind to the simplicity of the command. "Honoring" is not a term of affection but a term of sincerity. If a parent was a type two diabetic and the adult child began to notice symptoms of type two diabetes in their health, would it not be helpful to know the family history? Every first-time trip to a doctor involves a medical history. Honoring the parent shows the patterns of weakness that run in the genetics. The psychospiritual genetics are no less real, and being cognizant of them will help us stay committed to dealing with them, but it won't make them disappear. A more adolescent view of free will is more like to merely believe something away instead of acknowledging the challenge and the boundaries and help it will take to deal with it as an actual illness.

Before moving on, both *Great Expectations* and the ninth-grade standard *Romeo and Juliet* are illustrative of the fourth commandment's relevance today. Estella, Pip's obsession, gradually comes to understand that she is an unfeeling person because she has been raised to be so. She warns Pip that though she has feelings in a physical sense and understands when people speak of their feelings, she has none of her own. This realization comes to a head not with her relationship to Pip but with her adopted mother, Miss. Havisham. Ms. Havisham scolds her for being stock and stone and then is broken by Estella's response that she cannot love her. Estella's response is not a retort but a statement that she has been made this way and must be accepted as she has been made. It is Miss. Havisham's realization that she has made Estella her icy self even as she loved her that makes her sympathetic to Pip, as he is the one whose heart has been broken. Miss. Havisham's revenge on men, in general, had taken a focal point on Pip and would have continued until she realized that Pip was in the place where she was when she was left at the altar. This is where Dickens's view of honoring a parent and human evil supersedes Peck's model. By Peck's model, even when applying exorcism, the individual acting evilly must choose to renounce evil before beginning the healing process. Miss. Havisham is broken and then in the little time left begins to show sympathy and even empathy for Pip. Her brokenness and redemptive action precede any knowledge or act of the will regarding permission and understanding. And Estella herself is later broken by an abusive and financially irresponsible husband who uses up her wealth and breaks her spirit. When he dies, and years have passed, she can return to view what is left of Miss. Havisham's mansion, ironically named Satis House. Satis is a transliteration of the Latin word for "enough." Miss. Havisham's revenge was not enough. Estella's choice of a husband to gain independence was not enough, and even Pip's admission of his vanity is not enough as he goes back to an honest working life. There is, however, the issue of honor. If all these adults in the novel can learn to understand the cruelty of the adults who shaped them, surely it also could be said that this understanding took them away from the surroundings that were abusive. To remain near the abuse is to stay in the position of a child who is powerless. This is not honoring, and the commandment's promise of a long life is based on honor, not affection. So once again the pattern of a free life is based on the blunt promise that honoring parents will result in a long life. Before moving to the fifth commandment, it is helpful to look at Romeo and Juliet. The original play *Romeo and Juliet* is based on is a blunt warning for children and teenagers to listen to their parents or bear terrible consequences. Shakespeare, as he was so gifted at, takes this blunt morale and crafts a story full of multidimensional characters. However, it is adolescent impulsiveness that results in the eventual death of the two teen spouses. No matter how much the friar seems to desire the general welfare of the community and have some sort of lesson for Romeo to learn or how much the nurse seems to remember the heat of young love, their help is ultimately fatal. No matter how stuck in the feud the two families are, it has at least slowed the romance. This might have resulted in an eventual marriage and two very much alive spouses. The two families are not loving, but they are at least adults in their understanding that life and love are complicated. Romeo and Juliet are champions of free will, and the friar and the nurse—the two adults in a relationship with them—are also, particularly the friar, naïve enough to exercise free will on an idolatrous level and then attempt to blame providence when the plan fails. When parents are worth emulating, honor seems to make sense, but when they fall short or are even abusive, it makes it even more helpful to honor the spiritual and psychological genetics and exercise a plan that takes the tendencies and weaknesses seriously. To do otherwise is not only to break a commandment but to perhaps shorten both the physical life and the actual quality of life in the meantime. So, generation after generation of teenagers will mock their parents and then end up being their parents, and the cycle of the illusion of free will and the dishonoring of parents remains unbroken.

Chapter Six

The Most Obvious Commandment, Sort Of . . .

> You shall not murder.
>
> —EXOD. 20:13

Of all the commandments, this one seems the most obvious. True, there are others that are not exactly vague, but the average person on the street or in the hallways of a school doesn't usually has some sort of readymade rationale as to why this is OK. Even the arguments for self-defense and manslaughter aren't super hard to explain. The debate over the old King James translation of "Thou shalt not kill" and the subsequent arguments over capital punishment, abortion, and even veganism don't stick around once it is pointed out that the better translation is and always has been "Thou shalt not murder."[1] It isn't that the other points don't matter, but the initial debate is relatively quickly resolved. However, the fifth commandment has a distinct and inferred value that never goes away because human history is littered with violence, and violence leads to murder. If it doesn't always lead to murder, it is

---

1. https://www.gotquestions.org/you-shall-not-murder.html.

closer in so many more instances than we would like to admit. The United States has been involved in wars or armed combat for 222 of 239 years since 1776.[2] That's a staggeringly consistent ratio. It's estimated that there are at least forty documented armed conflicts going around the world right now. True, it would take an entire book or several books to differentiate between taking life in war and first-degree murder, so let's just move on. In the city of Chicago alone, over 530 people were killed this year. That's more than 100 fewer than the previous year[3], but it is staggering when you think that those numbers don't include people who died of old age or disease. So, murder is the culmination of so many other things—the increasing gap between the rich and the poor as well as institutional corruption and racial tensions. In Chicago, 76 percent of the homicide victims were African American,[4] and the city's government has long had corruption issues that have made it famous.

At this point, it becomes helpful to look again at the order of the commandments. Our general lack of focus leads us to worship things that aren't real, though they promise material wealth and comfort. Our high-school hallways are filled with kids self-medicating through technology, and gradually many who are at risk for various factors will lose the ability to self-medicate. When the music of the steady streams of videos can't calm, then what will? If the lack of ability to self-sooth becomes a violence issue, what are the risks of this escalating to severe levels that could even lead to murder? Yes, different cultures have different ways of expressing themselves in music, but when the music used to self-soothe glorifies violence, is the needed ability to focus placed on acts of violence? Does the instability of a home life added to the reality of being stuck in a job or jobs that require endless labor and no real rest produce hopelessness that can quickly turn to violence? The

---

2. Charpentier, Arthur "The U.S. has been at War 222 out of 239 Years" Freaknometrics.hypothesis.org. March 19, 2017.

3. Charles, Sam "Chicago's 2018 murder total falls for second straight year but still tops 530" Chicago Sun Times December 30, 2018.

4. Chicago Tribune. July 1, 2019

answer is of course yes, and the solutions are not simple. However, the commandments give a template for the boundaries of work, trust, and purpose that the distractions of Egypt, the endless sacrificing, and a life of bondage do not. Beyond that, the fifth commandment assumes culpability. It is that very assumption in terms of the word "murder," instead of killing, that has developed in our legal system so that we have degrees of murder in terms of how long it was a planned and understood action and manslaughter in terms of reckless behavior that resulted in the loss of life but was in no way intended. Cornelius Plantinga in his book *Not the Way It's Supposed to Be: A Breviary of Sin* explains the traditional Christian view.

Christians have traditional and plausibly reserved the word sin for culpable evil. The criterion of culpability distinguishes sin from certain natural evils, from simple errors and follies and especially from moral evils (kleptomania or necrophilia) that might have been blamelessly acquired. Thus, if Jim Bob (previously described White Supremacist) is not to be blamed for acquiring his racism, we can characterize his wrongful state of mind as moral evil, but not strictly speaking as sin, and we do not know that Jim Bob's is not, and because living in a no fault culture, we fear the softness of self-deception more than the hardness of accusation.

What Jim Bob's racism shows us is that moral evil is social as well as structural as well as personal: it comprises a vast historical and cultural matrix that includes traditions, old patterns of relationship and behavior, atmospheres of expectation, social habit.[5]

This description and outline of what has been called sin are helpful as we look at the fifth commandment, particularly in the cases of capital punishment. Our legal system has multiple avenues of appeal, especially for violent crimes, because, at least in theory, life is seen as sacred. Both sides of the capital punishment make their arguments, for or against, based on that presupposition. What Plantinga explains is helpful to understand, in that violence, though it may have a pinpoint in the action of one, has multiple

---

5. Plantinga, Cornelius Jr. *Not the Way It's Supposed To Be: A Breviary of Sin*. Wm. B. Eerdmans Publishing Company 1995.

shaping influences and as a result numerous culpable points. It may well be that the commandment is blunt and without qualification because who knows how many points of control-and-counter education are involved in a life that ends in the intentional taking of another life. The commandment may be blunt because it assumes culpability in human nature and, as a result, creates a hard boundary that allows no exceptions regarding culpable life-taking. To take a softer approach might bring so many exceptions or requirements into the argument that no conclusion would be reached. Early on in his work, Plantinga defines sin as the vandalism of shalom. The term "shalom" is Hebrew and is translated as peace. However, the translation, as explained by both rabbis and ministers, implies harmony, not just a cease-fire. So an unjust society will lead to violence and abuse, which will culminate in death, even culpable death that we know as murder.

One final note on murder, before moving to the sixth commandment: It precedes the prohibitions against theft, adultery, and coveting for strikingly logical reasons. It is the final extreme of all of those and the least socially acceptable. It is, however, the path of violence that precedes and ends containing all the others along its road to destruction. Daisy Buchanan, Jay Gatsby's obsession, is a strikingly shallow person. Her voice and very frame are light and airy. Gatsby's fantasy seems to have more depth and breadth than the real Daisy. When Daisy finally decides in front of Gatsby, the man she loves, not to leave her husband, it is Daisy who drives home and kills Myrtle. Gatsby covers for the crash and eventually yet unknowingly is wrongfully killed by Myrtle's husband, George, who in one final act of manipulation frames Gatsby. This speed soap opera of an ending brings murder into a remarkably shallow footing. Suddenly it doesn't look as severe as the questions of what about taking a life in war or in defense of our home and family from an intruder. Suddenly it is no more than what about covering for an emotional afternoon of having an affair exposed. What if our reasons for excusing violence are overly individualized? Honestly, like Daisy, Gatsby, and Tom, we quickly condone even the most violent of actions when it causes us personal pain or even inconvenience.

Chapter Seven

The Other Commandment Everyone Knows and Tells Stories About

Thou Shalt not Commit Adultery

—EXOD. 20:14

In ancient Canaan, the god Baal, a rather generic term for the head god, was both a favorite deity in Egypt and a god of fertility throughout the areas around Egypt. Like Osiris, there is intrigue in his myths regarding his lordship and violence within his family against him. There is also a recurring theme of resurrection, albeit temporary. Encyclopedia Judaica makes the Baal cult the rival and oppositional force to the beliefs of the ancient Hebrews.

Biblical narrative incorporates tales of Baal worship into the traditions of the wilderness wandering, thus tracing Baal worship to the earliest period of Israel's existence. At Shittim they attached themselves to Baal Peor, ate sacrifices for the dead, and indulged in sacred sexual orgies (Num. 25:1–11; Ps. 106:28). Life in a land dependent on rainfall enhanced the appeal of the Baal cult, and its pervasive influence persisted through the centuries, as the unrelenting protests of the prophets and the sporadic efforts at reform

THE OTHER COMMANDMENT EVERYONE KNOWS

attest. Horrendous and repulsive aspects of the worship—sexual excesses and perversions (Isa. 57:3–10), perhaps including copulation with animals (Hos. 13:2) such as Baal himself performed in the Ugaritic myth—are depicted in the prophetic tirades. Virtually all reference to Baal's consort, the violent "Virgin Anath"—with whom Baal copulates by the thousand in one of the Ugaritic mythological fragments—has been excluded from the Bible, but the goddesses Ashtart (Judg. 2:13) and Asherah (Judg. 6:30; II Kings 16:32–33) are associated with him.[1]

That pretty much sums up the open, violent approach to sexuality in the ancient mythologies. Norse and Greek mythologies are fairly replete with such stories. The players change, but the game stays the same. Monotheism stands in contrast, right from the first two commandments excluding multiple gods who demanded numerous sacrifices and had various orgy-like ceremonies to the third through fifth commandments that end in a prohibition against violence. So, it isn't an accident that ancient mythologies also required human sacrifice; there seems to be no end to the ancient deities' appetites, and they reflect gods made in the darkest images of what humanity is capable of in matters of sex and violence. So, the Hebrew God demands singular commitment and restricts sexuality to a single person. Hence, the commandment against adultery is a commandment against polytheism and fertility cults as well. The recurring biblical theme of infidelity is from this point on directly connected to the worship of other gods.

In our present age, we might find ancient worshipers to be vulgar, yet our current debates over the continued validity of marriage and our obsession with adultery in our music, movies, and books make the ancient world seem not as far from us as we might suppose. In the Grantchester mystery novel *Sidney Chambers and the Shadow of Death*, James Runcie's mystery-solving priest Sidney Chambers finds himself drawn to the mysterious murder of a man who was having not one but two affairs simultaneously. Ironically, though the wife is at one point a suspect, she has nothing to do with the murder. The first affair, with a secretary, is superseded by

---

1. Encyclopedia Judaica. Gale Group 2008

the second affair with a friend's wife whose position in high society and elegant looks make her worth running off with instead of just sneaking around with. Pamela Morton, the high-society second affair, turns off Sidney with her nonchalant attitude toward the wife. Upon asking Mrs. Morton why she didn't care for the women in Mr. Staunton's life (Staunton is the dead philanderer), Pamela Morton's reply is to ask why she should care about those women when they didn't make Mr. Staunton happy. The combination of Mrs. Morton's indifference toward the other women and her arrogance makes her a character that elicits no sympathy.

In addition, Mrs. Morton's use of Tupperware as an analogy for keeping things fresh and separate seems to be genuinely plastic in its applications and empathy. In the end, her affair isn't a secret, but she has no idea about the first one.[2] In the end, she is nearly killed by the first woman, and both of them are not any more sympathetic than Daisy or Tom Buchanan was in *The Great Gatsby*. Still the story reveals part of the nature of adultery. Mr. Staunton is a man who struggles with what seems to be a sort of depression, looking for sympathy and inspiration. His dalliance with his secretary turns out to be a fatal attraction that he doesn't see coming because of her status and easy conquest. Pamela Morton is more of an inspirational move, and his promise to run away with her seems more of a peak in the ups and downs of his life. If I were tempted to apply some sort of feminist critique of this story, the secretary would be the regional goddess while the more stately and cold Pamela Morton would be more of a Pantheon goddess in her icy indifference. Just the same, it leads not only to the death of a marriage but also to a murder. So, the sixth and seventh commandments remain connected by bonds of jealousy and passion—people sacrificing themselves, their security, and even their sanity in an attempt to maintain an elusive ecstasy. Indeed the orgies of a pagan cult are never too far away from the motives of a love triangle.

---

2. Runcie, James. *Sidney Chambers and the Shadow of Death*. Bloomsbury 2012

However, the debased actions of Runcie's story are also not likeable. The neurotic secretary; the cruel, high-society woman; and the drunk philanderer all seem to have some sort of a certain moment that makes their actions more easily condemnable. But what about when those who break marital vows seem more sympathetic? What about characters who aren't faithful but love each other?

However, much like impersonal deities of the ancient world, who demand without personal attachment, the characters of *Fences* are left with loss, sacrifice, and something less than a God whom they feared and put their trust in at the same time. Troy himself, even as he demands loyalty from his world, collapses as a man who chose the feeling of freedom, the affair itself, but lives with bondage and consequence, the loss of his wife's love even as they live under the same roof. Alberta, the woman Troy has an affair with, is never shown in the play, because she is not a complete character. Troy may not see himself as using her, but her absence seems to lessen her humanity, as she has a child with another woman's husband and dies in childbirth. Hers is in many ways a loss of self as well, a selfish act of being used, along with the ultimate loss, her life itself. Both women are sacrificed in a real and symbolic way. Alberta is never portrayed as younger or more attractive than Rose. That sort of portrayal, the ancient concubine or modern mistress, is absent form the story. Alberta functions as a way for Troy to forget his commitments and loss of dreams. She is no more a three-dimensional character than Daisy Buchanan is, although Fitzgerald chooses to show Daisy as a significant character. Daisy's two-dimensionality comes from her shallow materialist nature, while Alberta's absence only hammers home her place as an object.[3]

Wilson's portrayal of adultery is blunt and painful, with no glossing over of the consequences and complexities of the pain that comes from breaking marital vows. It may well be one of the most profound portrayals of human frailty in American literature, but I would be remiss, even dishonest, if I didn't turn to Nathaniel

---

3. August Wilson Fences.

Hawthorne's *The Scarlet Letter* before moving on from the sixth commandment. In the three characters of *The Scarlet Letter*, Hawthorne displays the full range of human frailty and the cost of redemption for each person involved in the breaking of marital vows.

First, there is Hester, the protagonist who takes center stage immediately in the novel. She is on the pillory, subjected to public humiliation because of her pregnancy, childbirth, and an unnamed father. Unlike some feminist portrayals of her, Hester is anything but heroic. She is defiant in her refusal to name the father but otherwise seems to suffer a level of stress that touches on the neurotic and affects the health and stability of her infant. Hester suffers in silence throughout the novel as she is judged over and over by a community that Hawthorne's considerable writing skill shows as brutally self-righteous. Hester herself is a mix of weakness and strength, at once showing loyalty but also showing a blind spot for a man who will not defend her even as she shields him. If anything, our modern sentiments would say Hester cares too much. She carries more of the relationship regarding responsibility even as the connection between her and Reverend Dimmesdale is a secret from the community at large. Ironically, Hester is a rescuer though she herself is guilty of adultery. Hawthorne allows his readers to be impressed with not just Hester's beauty but her perseverance and her loyalty. This invitation by the author to look upon a strong woman in a fallen state is reinterpreted by later readers. In a National Public Radio (NPR) article, titled "Hester Prynne: Sinner, Victim, Object, Winner," author Andrea Seabrook traces different interpretations of Hester's character. In the article, Professor Jamie Barlowe of the University of Toledo points out the growing feminist movement and argues that Hester was Hawthorne's contribution to a growing number of women who break societal boundaries. The other voice of the article is author John Updike who states:

> Hester is such an arresting and slightly ambiguous figure. She's a funny mix of a truly liberated, defiantly sexual woman, but in the end a woman who accepts the

penance that society imposed on her. And I don't know; I suppose she's an epitome of female predicaments.[4]

Updike finishes his point and the article by arguing that Hester is a mythic version of every woman's attempt to integrate her sexuality with societal demands. Updike and Barlowe have valid points to make about the role of women and the ambiguities in Hester's character, but they both seem to be ambivalent about the issue of adultery. It seems valid that there are double standards in the treatment of women in the novel as in most cultures, but the point of unfaithfulness is still the crucible of the book. Hester is not the most convincing Puritan, but she hardly fits a defiant, arrogant figure like Mrs. Morton. She is genuinely loyal but, frankly, a very awkward mother who struggles to love her daughter, Pearl. As the novel progresses, Hester seems to ultimately want to just run away with the man she loves. She has a flight more than fight reflex. In some ways, Hester has some of the qualities of Rose but does not display Rose's strength or self-awareness. Nowhere does Hester explain her weaknesses and what she's learned the way Rose does, but she does exhibit one trait tied strongly to adultery, the desire to continue the affair despite incredible consequences. Hawthorne's Hester is a woman who has put so much faith in the relationship with Dimmesdale that it has become her sole hope, her image of happiness. Even after Dimmesdale's confession and imminent death, Hester asks him if they will be together in the next world, having ransomed each other's souls. His response does not excuse his cowardice but shows the boundary of the commandments and the concern of the moral laws for the people rather than the people's supposed status and artificial purity.

It is, in fact, the character and demise of Dimmesdale that through Hawthorne's considerable writing skill binds the fallen minister to Hester not only in the plot but also in the existential question of the nature of breaking the seventh commandment and its consequences on the souls of those who cross its moral barrier. Dimmesdale raises the problem of those who know better, believe

4. Seabrook, Andrea. "Hester Prynne: Sinner, victim, object, winner." NPR. March 2008

in a moral boundary, and cross it with full knowledge unlike Hester who, despite significant strengths, is still driven by an emotional image of what she thinks Dimmesdale is rather than what he has done. Dimmesdale, on the other hand, lives with gutting guilt that is eating him alive. The narrative seems to demonstrate that he saw the good in Hester but could not keep himself from her. In this sense, it would seem that a modern critique would see his weakness as the by-product of a negative belief system that is anti-pleasure and keeps good people apart. However, that critique misses the point that Dimmesdale, even in his weakness, is governed by a moral law based on that which not ought to be. C. S. Lewis in his book *The Abolition of Man* argues that a modern approach to morality, which debunks the oughts as created, gets it thinking backward. Breaking a moral law is based on what works. The commandment against adultery is just as blunt and unqualified as the others, but the rest of Scripture and literature, in general, make excuses like "It just happened" or "I didn't mean it to happen" fly in the face of all the work it takes to keep such things secret. Even the most hedonistic adolescent at least has the reflex to keep such actions secret. So, if it is not a big deal, why hide it? There are those who do not attempt to hide cheating, but even their supposed openness is a pretty hard sell. So, Dimmesdale does lie to himself or at least justifies himself even though Hester is hardly some wanton temptress. Once again Lewis is instructive when he talks about the tension between reasoned faith and emotion.

> It is not reason that is taking away my faith: on the contrary, my faith is based on reason. . . . The battle is between faith and reason on one side and emotion and imagination on the other.[5]

A second example he gives is of a man with a pretty girl. "When he finds himself with her his mind loses its faith in that bit of knowledge and he starts thinking 'Perhaps she'll be different this time', and once more makes a fool of himself and tells her something he ought not have told her." And so, once again, "His

---

5. Lewis, C. S. *The Abolition of Man*. Collier Books 1947.

senses and emotions have destroyed his faith in what he knows to be true."

So immediately it's worth clarifying that Hester is, in general, an honest person, but both of them are driven by their emotional connection rather than any sort of realization, much less admission of the disastrous consequences of their secret union and Hester's public punishment. However, it can't be overstated that Hester is grossly irrational in both protecting Dimmesdale and taking all the punishment on herself.

The romantic outcry would be to say that she does all she does because of love. That sort of love doesn't heal Hester or raise Dimmesdale to the kind of manhood that would admit his part and take some of Hester's shame away. That is because the lie they both cling to seems to be genuinely held by Hester and allowed by Dimmesdale. Dimmesdale and Hester eventually do plan to run away together, start over in a paradise of their own making, but one man stops them and creates a climax occasionally equaled but never surpassed in American literature and perhaps the ultimate overlap between the commands not to murder and not to commit adultery.

The person and what becomes of the person of Roger Chillingworth is perhaps Hawthorne's intentional or unintentional melding of the sixth and seventh commandment, inverted in the person of someone who has crossed a moral boundary and moved further on toward damnation. Chillingworth is the embodiment of the damage that can happen to someone who has been cheated on. Truthfully, there are many examples of women who have been cheated on who become bitter or continue what Stewart Van Leeuwen talks about when she discusses women who continue pursuing men. That pursuit could be of the man who cheats or of another man who had the same issues. In such a case, a woman could repeat the same relationship with a different person. In Chillingworth, we are confronted with a person who has some degree of self-knowledge but becomes so obsessed with punishing Dimmesdale, his wife's lover, that he loses his humanity. On a literary level, Chillingworth is somewhat flat, lacking in empathy for others from the beginning. He, however, is not devoid of understanding. He admits to Hester that they were poorly matched because of the age difference between them and his introverted, bookish ways. He, even upon hearing Hester acknowledge that he as the cheated-upon party has been the most wronged, states that it is too late. His admission is a clue as to the narrative's view of the moral law. True, Chillingworth has been cheated on and is in some ways the victim of the breaking of the sixth commandment. He, however, in seeking revenge is very guilty of a type of violence that also crosses the barrier of prohibiting murder. In an article in *Psychology Today*, therapist Karyn Hall writes an article, titled "Revenge: Will You Feel Better?" She addresses multiple studied looks at revenge but also comments on revenge as perceived justice and the pleasure of getting back at someone. It isn't hard to understand why someone who has been wronged would see the need to rebalance the situation. However, in the same article, neuroscientist Dan Arely shows that PET scans of people thinking about revenge had a higher activation level of the striatum (center of the brain) where pleasure is felt. It didn't even matter if the person thinking about revenge was the person wronged; the pleasure was felt by just thinking about revenge.[6] So, it may be that setting things right or some view of justice is either naïve or easily hijacked by the pleasure we take in planning revenge. Hall speaks candidly toward the end of the article about warning against retaliation, as the actual acts of revenge don't bring the same sensations of pleasure and often make a difficult situation even more complicated. This is the issue with Chillingworth who becomes fiendish in not only punishing Dimmesdale but also takes pleasure in his victim's slow demise. The naming of Chillingworth as a leech is a clear double meaning going beyond the medical term of that time and describing the moral state of the man who lives off another. This is then a theft of life, slowly removing and damming the soul of the taker, which leads us to the eighth commandment.

6. Hall, Kary Phd. "Revenge: *Will You Feel Better? Psychology Today* September 15, 2013.

Chapter Eight

The Commandment We Quibble Over the Most

You shall not steal.

—EXOD. 20:15

PERHAPS the eighth commandment isn't as scandalous as the sixth, for our modern world is obsessed with sex, but surely this command is no less apparent, though all commandments seem to come with provisos and excuses built into the way we read them. However, the excuses offered to justify theft are quite easily dealt with. What about the man who steals to feed his family because of poverty? What about the man or woman who steals insulin for her diabetic mother because they can't afford the insurance to pay for it? No matter how emotionally we speak these qualifications, they don't answer the question of theft. The man who suffers from poverty may have been stolen from being given an honest wage. Or sadly, he may have wasted what he has through one sort of addiction or another. We often don't know, but theft isn't just because of need. The Hebrew scripture anticipates our arguments: "Men do not despise the thief if he steals to satisfy his hunger. Yet if caught, he must pay sevenfold; he must give up all the wealth of his house." To us, this may sound harsh, but it isn't a command; it is a proverb. It doesn't give an ultimatum but rather pronounces the most consistent observation. The observation is that most people don't judge a thief who steals out of poverty or despair, but theft is still not good. Langston Hughes's classic short story *Thank You, Ma'am* recounts the story of a boy who is caught trying to steal the purse of an older woman. In the way that only a strong woman of color can, the woman grabs him in return and pulls him to her apartment. There we realize that the boy who didn't have money for blue suede shoes was attempting to steal from a woman who cooks on a hot plate because she doesn't own a stove. She cooks the boy dinner and, then upon being asked, if he is going to be taken to jail, delightfully and seriously, states, "I've done things I wouldn't tell anyone, things I wouldn't tell God if he didn't know." The boy, Roger, moves to where he can be seen as she prepares dinner because "he did not trust the woman not to trust him. And he did not want to be mistrusted now."[1] The beauty of the story is not that we needed to be taught that some children steal because of poverty but rather that despite stealing, being wrong, grace, mercy, and honesty are still the salves for the world of theft. The old woman tells the boy after she gives him money for the shoes that he can ask her next time. The boy, though he cannot bring himself to say the words, leaves a genuinely grateful person who will be both a barrier against theft and a motivator to live honestly.

Having said that gratitude and honesty are the counters against theft, it still needs to be stated that we are often quick to judge the small thief, the one driven by illiteracy and occasionally violence. On the other hand, our materialism often gives shelter and even solace to the rich thief, the one who has no need to steal but is driven by the perpetual desire for more. Joy Davidman in her book *Smoke on the Mountain* writes of the eighth commandment and our willingness to excuse theft if it is in the acquisition of wealth.

---

1. Hughes, Langston. *Thank You Ma'am*. https://civics.sites.unc.edu

For the age of capitalism, a hundred years ago, did maintain that wealth was the reward and the proof of virtue. And that money-making methods were too Holy for a government to regulate. The argument reached its ugly conclusion. In negro slavery; both the New England ship captains who traded in slaves and Southern Planters who owned them defended themselves with Old Testament. Phrases about the sons of Ham being predestined bondservants. So often have Ancient Hebrew savageries have been used by certain Protestants to cloak them. Offenses that one might paraphrase Dr. Johnson by saying that the Old Testament is the last refuge of scoundrels.[2]

Honestly, for theft on a grand scale to take place, all that is needed is a more significant profit margin. One of my college professors used to say "Money covers a multitude of sins." So, in our modern wealthy, technologically advanced societies, we differentiate between white- and blue-collar crime. Bernie Madoff, chairman of the Nasdaq, in 1990, pulled off for years the largest Ponzi financial scheme in US history. Madoff used what has been called the "split strike conversion strategy" and then just deposited his clients' money into a single account, paying his clients when they wanted out of the investment. Even with prison time as a very real consequence, Madoff stated, "Everybody was greedy, everybody wanted to go on, and I just went along with it."[3] One has to wonder if he is at least partially right and was one of the people who got caught rather than the only one who was guilty. In either case, what Davidman goes on to write about is that theft today may be defined as a way of getting something for nothing that makes us as vulnerable to stealing as the kid who shoplifts. And since Davidman is no doubt correct in identifying wealth as something we acquaint with virtue, stealing is a particular weakness for those who are good at acquiring wealth. Also, since wealth seems to be a result of virtue in the minds of so many, it should not be surprising that what has been called the prosperity gospel is undoubtedly the

2. Davidman, Joy. *Smoke On the Mountain*. Westminster Press. 1954

3. Bernard Madoff: remorse, tears and a good character reference from his therapist. theguardian.com February 28, 2011

American heresy. Karen Spears Zacharias in her book *Will Jesus Buy Me A Double-Wide? Cause I Need Room for My Plasma TV* explores the world of prosperity but, in fairness, begins with references to our pop culture and its obsession with secrets to wealth. In fact, in the opening pages of her book, Spears Zacharias tells of walking through an airport in Utah looking at the best sellers in the bookstore and finding a book titled *The Secret*, a motivational text that sells the idea that those who show forth good energy will attract wealth and happiness because that's just how the universe works. Then Spears Zacharias goes on to laugh at her daughter's iPod selection from Destiny's Child that equates that positive things lead to prosperity. Of course it's not clear what is meant by "things" so the ambiguity and promise is even more vague. On and on, the list goes with prosperity preachers taking money from those who want faith; healing; and, of course, happiness. If these accounts seem like heresy, consider that Joel Osteen, pastor of the massive Lakewood Church in Houston, has a net worth between $40 and $60 million. He lives with his family in a seventeen-thousand-square-foot mansion, worth an estimated $10.5 million in River Oaks.[4] His wife Victoria Osteen has been quoted as saying from the pulpit:

> When we obey God; we're not doing it for God; we're doing it for ourselves. Do good for yourself. Do it because God wants you to be happy. When you come to church when you worship Him, you're not doing it for God, really—you're doing it for yourself, because that's what makes God happy. Amen?[5]

In this surprisingly self-serving quotation, Osteen manages to combine the first two commandments with the eighth, making happiness the point of worship and our chief reason for going to church. If that sounds like we worship ourselves and our image of happiness, it's because that is what that means. And if our

---

4. Farrow, Emma. Joel Osteen House: What He goes Home to is Inspiring velvetropes.com.

5. Slick, Matt. Victoria Osteen says to do Good for YOurself, not God. carm.org

THE COMMANDMENT WE QUIBBLE OVER THE MOST

happiness is measured in our wealth, then it wouldn't be hard to see how tempting it would be to acquire that wealth. The dumbed-down version of this walks down the hallway with a Money over Everything T-shirt refusing to listen to teachers or counselors because they don't make enough money. The Osteens of the world wouldn't wear such T-shirts, but their system of thought and lavish lifestyle is grounded in such a philosophy of life. So, what can be said for a culture that exalts wealth to a godlike status and then sets itself up for the illicit taking of possessions from others and calling it anything but stealing? Well, though it is hardly a comfort, we didn't come up with the idea, and the concept of theft and prohibitions against it are universal. Though the prosperity gospel is our heresy, other cultures can communicate the strength of the eighth commandment. So before moving on to the ninth commandment, I move to Khaled Hosseini's modern classic *The Kite Runner*. Early in the novel, the protagonist Amir gets a lesson from his father, a man of high prestige and prowess.

> "Good," Baba said, but his eyes wandered. "Now, no matter what the mullah teaches, there is only one sin, only one. And that is theft. Every other sin is a variation of theft. Do you understand that?" "No, Baba Jan," I said, desperately wishing I did. I didn't want to disappoint him again. [. . .] "When you kill a man, you steal a life," Baba said. "You steal his wife's right to a husband, rob his children of a father. When you tell a lie, you steal someone's right to the truth. When you cheat, you steal the right to fairness. Do you see?" [. . .]
>
> "There is no act more wretched than stealing, Amir," Baba said. "A man who takes what's not his to take, be it a life or a loaf of *naan* . . . I spit on such a man. And if I ever cross paths with him, God helps him. Do you understand?"[6]

Baba's definition of sin is the eighth commandment explained. His connection of the evil that comes with it is pretty much flawless logic. A lie is stealing the truth, murder is stealing a life,

---

6. Hosseini, Khaled. *The Kite Runner*. Riverhead Books 2003.

cheating is stealing the right to fairness, and so on. By this logic, you basically could define all evil, and as a result, it not only shows the problem with stealing but also the nature of sin and moral law. Of course, as those who have read the novel know, Baba commits adultery with his friend and servant's wife and, as a result, cannot fully raise the child as his own. This revelation comes to Amir after Baba's death and causes him to see his entire life as a lie. His father stole another man's wife and, in covering his sin, took the truth from his son. This definition and fleshing out of what stealing is and does to people goes beyond the arguments we raise over unjust societies and who is stealing. As Joy Davidman points out, we do not want to look at the thief in the mirror. Baba is a powerful example of a man trying to atone for what he has done. Amir is a powerful example of a son who lives in his father's significant shadow and eventually finds out his father wasn't invulnerable but very human. Humanity leans in the direction of theft. For Baba, it was another man's wife and the incomplete narrative he gives to Amir about having a half-brother. Amir's half-brother, Hassan, grows up with him as his playmate but is the son of his father's chief servant. So, the pattern of the rich stealing from the poor is much clearer when the reader finds out what the actual connections were and not just what they appeared to be. However, in his betrayal of Hassan, Amir sees that he is like his father in the sense of not having lived up to what he should have done. Though he is different in many ways, he finds himself the same in the betrayal of a friend and brother. The final part of the novel are built upon Amir traveling back to Afghanistan to save his friend and brother Hassan's son. The ending is not Disneyesque in that the violence that took Hassan's life is visited in many of the same ways on his son, but Amir finds him and bears the extreme cost of redemption in bringing him back to America as his own son. In truth, Amir cannot give back what he stole from his friend—loyalty and standing with him instead of hiding. Baba cannot give back his friend's dignity in having taken his wife. However, Baba's building of an orphanage shows his desire to help all children even though he cannot fully claim his biological child. Amir's adoption of Hassan's son is an example of redeeming a debt he owes for having stolen the loyalty he should have shown. The tangled lies tied to the stealing of others and what should have been extended to others show the connection between words and truth and the damage we can do when we don't heed the eighth commandment.

Chapter Nine

The Easiest Commandment to Break?

> You shall not bear false witness against your neighbor.
> —EXOD. 20:16

For a long time, I remember this commandment was used against gossip. Somewhere around my college years, I remember being told it was actually closer to perjury. This was because what we call swearing is actually profanity as opposed to an oath. In the ancient world, oaths carried much more weight than our swear to God makeshift statements. We do put our hand on the Bible before testifying, so the perjury is closer. In what initially seems tongue-in-cheek but is actually quite right, Joy Davidman points out that "primitive men who killed and raped and looted without a second thought regarded a false oath as an offense against the gods and looked with superstitious horror for a bolt of lightning to strike the blasphemer dead."[1]

This point brings the commandment from perjury to false prophecy since swearing by the gods was blasphemy, which was punishable by death. Words were the primary means of

---

1. Davidman. See Note xl above.

distinguishing the sacred and, as a result, were not thrown around as carelessly as we do today. Take, for example, today's use of Twitter. Harsh and unfounded accusations can be leveled so quickly that what once would have landed you in court may well get you more followers. Where once my grandparent's generation read the paper or listened to the radio for the news, only moving to television in their later years, now we have twenty-four-hour news. In fact, there are so many news sources that you can watch what you want to watch, where interpretation precedes event. So, to some extent, our news cycle with its continuous spin is a sort of secular prophetic cycle, interpreting, predicting, but not really having any consequence for being wrong in its predictions. In fact, the explosion of social media over the past few years has recreated the pillory in a sense that each person's missteps or even misquotes can be trolled and viewed in seconds. True, the pillory was brutal in its public humiliation, but there was a trial and conviction before being put to the scaffold. Today, the prosecution is so subjective that the sentence and pillory can be shared on the Internet for hours before the convicted subject knows of their conviction or what they were initially accused of. Think of how many hours a day are spent by teens on their phones. Those same high-school students will complain that there isn't enough time to do their work or that their classes are boring. Not long ago, after a seminar on an article we read, titled "'Quixote,' Colbert and the Reality of Fiction,"[2] I asked several of my students why they thought it was funny that Don Quixote did crazy things. They replied that something about it was so exaggerated that it was funny, but the violence was obviously so hyperbolic that it couldn't have been real. I asked if any of them had been to India. They said no, and I admitted I had never been there either. I followed by asking them how they knew what it looked like if they had never been there. Immediately, they reached for their phones. (Sometimes it's too easy.) I interjected, wanting to know if the pictures on their phone could be doctored. They laughed because my generation was dependent on Photoshop and

---

2. Egginton, William. Quixote, Colbert and the Reality of Fiction. New York Times September 25, 2011.

cutting and editing, whereas theirs could create whole scenes that had never existed. So, when I asked them again if they believed there was an India because of what they had seen on their phone, the trap had been set and sprung. In a journal, following the class, one girl said she had never thought how many things she'd just accepted because she could look them up on her phone. We know through elections and scandals that people on TV, radio, and the Internet lie and make money off of lying. However, with more and more dependence on phones, it may be that bearing false witness is becoming less of a broken commandment through words and has moved to pictures. It's as if the speed we demand from our devices will permanently outdistance the content of what we perceive as truth. We doubt facts and see reality as an impossibility and genuinely are guilty of bearing false witness with graven images, which outnumber any pagan pantheon.

Perhaps it is the speed at which we now access images that not only makes the prohibition against graven images so dangerous but also seems to combine its flaws most efficiently with the commandment against bearing false witness. The Internet does make the ability to pillory someone else much more comfortable, but the ability to misrepresent ourselves is also a monstrous aspect of the Internet, social media in particular. Like much of technology, the use of it is usually what people will say is the problem. Ask the question, and many adults and most adolescents will say that social media is neutral and that it's all about how it's used. Of course, that argument as a template could be used for all sorts of things, but I'll try to stick to social media until I have followed up my point. Bearing false witness, in a legal sense, is perjury. Perjury is lying under oath. An oath is giving one's word as a pact. At one time, this was considered sacred because it was bound by a reference to God, and it was understood that words had consequences. Today, it is easy to prove that words, even or especially false words, have consequences.

I remember the first time, several years ago, that a student shared that she had found a fake website with pictures of her and all sorts of salacious lies on it. I still remember that the school's principal as well as the resource officer got involved in getting it taken down. On another occasion, a website had been set up, but this person had more skill, and the site stayed up for a while, and the perpetrator wasn't immediately, if ever, found. Still another girl was subject to brutal verbal assaults online, and the resource officer took digital pictures to obtain a restraining order against a volatile ex-boyfriend. Yes, all three of these victims were girls, and two of the three perpetrators were also girls. In the ancient world, temple prostitutes were expected to spend their lives in service of those who needed a blessing from the gods. It's amazing that when someone is victimized, it is more likely to be a girl, and in spite of empowering women as a society, we have also had a rise in violence of women against women. While teaching the pillory scene from *The Scarlet Letter*, I asked my students once if it was believable that the women in the audience were harsher to Hester than the men, even the men who had passed the legal judgment on her. One very smart and precocious young lady said yes. When I asked her what the difference was between male and female judgment, she stated that a guy could judge you or even hit you in the face, but a girl could ruin your life.

Also, as the Internet has given everyone a voice, being an authority means significantly less. I used to use the CDC website for an essay project on who smoked more in society. The main area of the study showed that more people who are classified as poor smoke than those who are classified as rich. The study showed that wealthy people in the United States not only drank more expensive alcoholic beverages but also drank more in quantity. Over the three years that I gave this assignment, it became less and less effective because students didn't want to accept the claims of the CDC studies. They thought the site could be making things up, or they thought it wasn't any more accurate than any other sites they might have found. This curious combination of not trusting the Internet and believing what you as an individual can find combined with the final factor of believing personal opinion over everything made research-based writing extremely difficult. However, if there is a prohibition against bearing false witness, this pattern I found in my students is believable and even predictable. We don't trust what we see online, because we don't trust language. We don't trust what we find online because although we prefer images to words, we know they can be altered. And yet, many teens struggle with self-esteem issues bordering on and crossing over into the suicidal because they find what others have presented online to be more attractive, confident, and alluring than what they see around them. The truth is nothing on social media is new. Adolescents, and I mean that as a state, not just a stage, have the constant effect of self-concept by worrying about what others are thinking. It's more acute in teenagers because it's natural to worry about how you're perceived when you are beginning to individuate. The process tends to prolong when you don't form several real beliefs. The cyberworld of social media takes the normal adolescent traits and tendencies and doesn't allow any regrets for the teenager or any other mind. So instead of walking the hallways of your school worrying about how you look or more specifically what others think of how you look, you spend more time looking at your phone, seeing other projections of what they want to be perceived as in a never-ending loop. On top of that, you participate in that loop, looking for positive feedback in the form of comments, shares, and likes. It's a never-ending cycle without a Sabbath, and since you aren't physically interacting with others, the risk of bearing false witness against others or you are high. Also, since social media is driven by advertising, it stands to reason that the more the time that is spent on it the greater the chances that the individual is left open to marketing strategies as a target rather than as an individual in a relationship. The difference is that the primary purpose of a marketing target is to get the target to buy products or in the case of the Internet to purchase and to visit sites that market various products. So, individuals are limited to cyber beings who have multiple tendencies, likes, and dislikes. A recent study shows that teens who increase their time on social media have stronger tendencies to look at others in judgmental ways that move actively upward or downward. Being a teenager tends to be a more judgmental time of life anyway, but the spike in judgment also is tied to marketing, which works off impulses. (Teenagers are neurologically proven to be more vulnerable to weaker impulse control.)[3] Couple this with the increase in time spent online in general, and things like facts and truth become extremely relative unless you can specify what something is relative to. For example, written language is relative to the culture and period it is used in. The amount in a paycheck is relative to the general cost of living and spending habits of the individual. However, in the teen mind and in the state of adolescence that we can all fall into, the "relative to what" question is so vague in its context but so specific to a million little opinions that it seems inevitable that we will continue to bear false witness in our judgment of others and in our presentation of ourselves. The grand illusion is that we can do so with fewer consequences because we are online. All this bearing of false witness, which is a form of lying, leads to insecurity, jealousy, and aggressive judgment. If you couple that with the consistent and perpetual marketing we all live under in our present materialistic society, you will inevitably move into the area of the tenth commandment.

3. B.J. Casey and Kristina Caudle. The Teenage Brain and Self Control cdps.sagepub.com April 1, 2013.

Chapter Ten

When It All Comes Together

You shall not covet your neighbor's house. You shall not covet your neighbor's wife, or his male or female servant, his ox or donkey, or anything that belongs to your neighbor.

—EXOD. 20:17

THE final commandment, like the second commandment, comes with examples. Just like not making graven images need examples of what people were doing at the time, so coveting needs examples of what not to covet—specifically, not the neighbor's wife, animals, or servants. True, as we have already looked at, graven images change over time, but the pattern stays the same. So, it is with coveting, though the categories are still quite accurate. Perhaps our cultural and technological advances haven't changed the areas where we tend to covet. The areas are spouses, those who serve our neighbors, and their possessions.

One of the more popular responses to this prohibition, whether it is realized or not, is a sort of downsizing. If having stuff breeds wanting stuff, which leads to eventually wanting what others have, then just stop wanting. This is a direct response to the idea that more stuff will make you happy. Wealth can give you some types of temporary pleasure, and it doesn't make anyone more enlightened to pretend that it doesn't. However, the acquisition is a fast-spreading disease, and coveting is part and parcel of the limitless desire to have more. Eventually, more doesn't just stay limited to what you can acquire but extends to taking what others have; it is endlessly amusing to see that the wealthy of our society are those who talk about downsizing. Jake Amerding in his song "Hipster Lullaby" croons, "It takes about a thousand bucks a night to live a life so free." It's easy to talk about the evils of materialism or even have some sort of Buddhist angle on not coveting that Hollywood seems to hold to. However, it is less than believable to talk about sharing and not get caught up in all the materialism when you live in massive mansions. What does seem plausible is that the more you get, the more you want, so coveting appears to be an upper-middle-class to wealthy sin. This doesn't mean that the poor can't covet. However, the acquisition isn't the same as survival. It may not be virtuous, but the person who is just trying to get by may long for things but is more used to having to give them up or do without them. Perhaps that might bring a temptation to steal or even to be bitter about the world, in general, but coveting is so attached to us and our society that the listing of it as last may be more about all the other ones building up to it this one weakness than leaving the least powerful one till the end. Aesop's fables contain the story of an envious and covetous man who is granted any wish by Zeus himself. The condition Zeus gives the man is that whatever he wishes for, his neighbor will receive twice as much. Aesop's fable concludes with the covetous man, unable to think of his neighbor having more, wishes to lose one of his own eyes to leave his neighbor blind. Joy Davidman points out the nature of the tenth commandment.

> The Tenth commandment is unique; its predecessors deal with specific actions, but this alone forbids a state of mind. It is the first implied awareness that wrong ideas precede wrong actions and that no matter how pious and decorous a man's outward behavior may be if he

encourages his mind to seethe with hate and greed, he is an abomination in the sight of God.[1]

Davidman's words are poignant but may catch today's reader off guard with the final phrase. Isn't that judgmental and harsh? Surely God is more loving than that? Consider that coveting cuts open the coveter from the inside and cuts into the coveted from the outside. It encourages and excuses all the other prohibitions. It isn't just a movie plot to plan the murder of someone because a person is coveting someone's spouse. Who doesn't love a great heist movie, but have you ever notice that the great thieves in these movies usually have an awful lot of wealth? The film *Oceans 12* is an excellent example of theft that comes from coveting and competition.

In summary, the original gang of super thieves, having spent much of their money, have been found out by the millionaire crook they stole from, and have to pull of another heist to pay their debts while competing against another master thief. All this brings about the romanticized ending where the tension between thieves, a policewoman who is also a love interest of Brad Pitt's con artist character, and her estranged thief father come together. The one part of all the clever plot twists is that theft is a battle of one-upmanship between really handsome and cool people. In a positive review for the *Chicago Sun-Times*, Roger Ebert gave the film three out of four stars and applauded its cleverness: "The movie takes inventory of its characters with the same droll wit it does everything else . . . The movie is all about behavior, dialogue, star power, and wiseass in-jokes. I really sort of liked it."[2] I tend to like witty films, so I get it, but all the dialogue and smooth thinking do bring up the reality that much of what we could call covetousness comes from competition rather than any sort of need. However, since competition is addictive, at some point, it becomes difficult to know when competition has become an addiction. Either way,

1. Davidman. See Note xl above.
2. Ebert, Roger. *Chicago Sun Times*. December 9, 2004.

competition in its unhealthy version is about taking from someone else, which is a functional definition of coveting.

Of course, our society has built an entire advertising enterprise that works off coveting. The old Pontiac commercial claimed, "Pontiac, we build excitement!" One could argue that they build cars, but that isn't as sexy. Speaking of sexy, cars have always been marketed with a sexy woman. The message was clear: the two go together. It isn't much of a jump to go from having a nice car and a girl to having a nice car, and taking someone else's girl. Years ago, Robin Leach hosted the show *Lifestyles of the Rich and Famous* giving tours of outrageously wealthy mansions and vacations of haute, rich celebrities for whom money was no object. Today, shows are perhaps more accessible as HGTV and have countless fixer-upper shows and reality series that are in many ways likeable advertisements where attractive people get other attractive, successful people to buy the home of their dreams or the ludicrously labeled "starter home." Whether a celebrity or just unrealistically labeled regular people, the message that you just need to buy another house or fix the one you have and happiness and success await is inferred. Those are the shows marketed to adults, but perhaps the most brazen embracing of coveting is advertising marketed toward children.

Children's back-to-school commercials are mostly about having the latest clothes and making an appearance. The first day of school is marketed as a red-carpet event. It isn't just clothes. What you take in your lunch should not only be what you want to eat, it should be what everyone else wants. Kids have traded food as long as there have been kids packing lunches. However, kids being told what they want and making sure that they have it is not a matter of taste but rather a matter of marketing. This creates a literal have and have-not situation because the kids have been told what would be fashionable to eat. So, school shopping becomes having the clothes everyone wants, eating what was advertised, and being seen. It's a setup for coveting but also, given the homogenizing of tastes to fit one particular look, it is also a combination of the tenth and the second commandments. So, the image is everything, and consequently, those who don't have are left coveting what others have while those who do have get the temporary just-opened feeling of superiority that lasts as long as the latest fashion. Since so much marketing is online, it stands to reason that much of our desires to have things are more suggestions of what we want than what we are being told to want. Regarding children, this creates coveting tied to a natural, even healthy, impulse. Children are often taught to listen to someone who is older. If it isn't their parents, it will be an older sibling, coach, teacher, or a grandparent. When advertising uses adults to tell children what they should want, they have taken something virtuous and replaced it with an order to buy, eat, or play with certain things. So, when children want things, the desire to have more and more leads to disappointment when it is realized that the present-opening event is over. So, by the time children have grown to adolescents, it is clear that getting things sometimes runs into others already having those things. Couple this with shows where the preteens look like adults and live out a soap-opera dramas, and the formula is perfect.

Now you can fashionably covet things and people. Joy Davidman was right when she wrote, "Can the best of us feel that he is not corrupted by 'dogma of increasing wants'?" She goes on to explain that most people compare themselves to rampant even abusive materialism while excusing their greed and covetousness. Incisively, Davidman points out that "but for what do we pray? Do we cry to dream again? Do we ask the Lord, not for Heaven but for a way of keeping the automobiles and television sets?" These words of Davidman were published in 1953, but they are just as accurate today. Perhaps we might add smartphones and whisper our prayers to Alexa for more convenience and stuff that can be sent straight to our door, provided that everyone else is keeping the eighth commandment and doesn't take our newest purchase off the front porch.

Chapter Eleven

Moving Forward, Wrapping Up

THE commandments do build up to our most adolescent and perhaps most common response to crossing moral boundaries. Hollywood and the Internet might tell us that our problems are mostly tied to sex or some sort of past trauma. Without underestimating those, it turns out that we are easily dissatisfied and look quickly to things to make other issues OK. At this point, commandments 1, 2, 7, 8, 9, 10 overlap in a multitude of ways. So why does sex catch our eye? Is it that we've bought into so much Freudianism or is it older than that? My final thoughts are that it is older than that. My final literary thoughts come from the book of II Samuel, *The Odyssey*, and Arthur Miller's *The Crucible*.

Odysseus, after surviving the Trojan War, turns homeward after insulting the gods. On the way, he lies to his crew to save himself and is kept as a lover first by Circe and then by Calypso. In the actual text of the Odyssey, it is unclear if Odysseus loses track of time because he is happy with Circe or if her powers as an enchantress bewitch him. Although the TV series is far inferior to the original work, the explanation Circe gives Odysseus as he lies in her bed is telling and helpful in understanding the consequences of crossing a moral boundary. "Poor Odysseus, you think you have been here five days when it's been five years. Here in my palace time has no meaning it passes slips by fades however I choose. What seemed like a day to you, an hour even a moment was a year outside these walls?"[1] Odysseus doesn't believe her in the film version until he is told to go out and see his ship buried under five years of sand and tide. Time in mythological stories is a great temptation, a chance to feel immortality and to indulge in sensual pleasures while still maintaining the idea of returning to the normal life left behind. In the Odyssey, this involves gods and mythological barriers. However, the gods of ancient Greece seem like super people, indulging in the most vacuous of moral patterns and simply showing our behaviors on a grand scale. The commandments don't tell us how to avoid temptation, but they clearly state where it is. Yes, Odysseus has committed adultery, and even though Hermes tells him, he can't resist Circe; he doesn't challenge the messenger or the message. However, it is Odysseus's pride that draws him to the point where he even reaches Circe's island. He lies to his men and doesn't acknowledge warnings from various divinities. True, the world view of the Greeks was not monotheistic, but *The Odyssey* still shows a human desire to fight against God's commands and still survive, even make it home like Odysseus. Perhaps Odysseus is the greatest Greek hero because he does escape the wrath of certain gods and does make it back to regain his family and kingdom. However, his entire crew dies as a result of his decisions, and he is unfaithful to his wife that costs him the time that Circe mocks him with. That combination of a moral boundary and the loss of time speaks volumes about human nature. Who doesn't assume, while they are bearing false witness, engaging in adultery, coveting, or even committing an act of violence that somehow time has stood still or the actions themselves are somehow frozen, separated from the rest of their lives? Perhaps this is why so many even speak of violations of trust as aberrations. The image of a scale fills so many cultures as if our lives were weighed by our deeds, both good and evil. However, who could honestly, despite our systematic efforts to excuse, believe that all our actions stack equally? Who can't think of a ten-year friendship shattered and discarded by one lie? Who

1. *The Odyssey*. Miniseries. Hallmark Entertainment 1997.

can't think of a marriage that spanned decades destroyed by one illicit relationship? Who can't think of a life driven by noble causes turned sour by a lapse of taking what was not theirs to secure success or take from what seemed a dangerous opponent? Our thefts, big and small, can launch the scale of morality in a direction that makes the consequences to those around us so violent that the idea of stacked and measured worth seem silly or diabolically foolish.

The ancient Hebrews' narratives are often fleshing out of all ten boundaries crossed, but perhaps none is more famous than David and Bathsheba. Maybe this is more because of our modern Freudian obsession with sex, but it does raise other issues that in truth weigh as heavily on the story's point as the parts that might more readily grab our attention. The story is relatively basic in its set up. David's troops are off at war in what the book of Samuel says is the time when kings went off to war. David, however, remains at the palace, a fairly sure sign of wealth and perhaps stagnation. Kings go off to war, but he doesn't. He sees a woman bathing while walking on the roof of his palace. This, in typical Hebrew understatement, fires quickly through a narrative that includes Bathsheba getting pregnant, her husband being set up to die on the battlefield to vote for the pregnancy, and the confrontation of David by the prophet Nathan. In one brief narrative, the reader is shown coveting, adultery, murder, and false witness of a man in power who attempts to cover himself. Nathan's confrontation in the form of a story is one of the most powerful passages in ancient scripture. Nathan enters the story late, telling the king he must tell him of injustice in his kingdom. Then he proceeds, in the middle of the king's court, to tell the story of a poor man who only owned a single lamb. After describing how that lamb was his unique joy, he speaks of a rich man who took the lamb and had it slaughtered for a banquet at his mansion. Upon hearing this, King David's anger burns white hot, and he interrupts saying that such a man, the man who would take from another, deserves to die. The trap has been set. David not only recognizes injustice but also feels and thinks strongly against it. Nathan's confrontation is complete when he says you are that man. David has taken from someone else in the act of coveting, committed adulterous theft, and covered it with violence. David repents in sincerity, but the rest of the narrative is fraught with violence and court intrigue that come directly and indirectly from David's relationships and his competing children. The story doesn't clean up its characters and doesn't take away the consequences of crossing boundaries even as it gives the reader almost poetic confessions languishing over personal sins. Unlike Odysseus, the divine intervention doesn't provide extra powers to the leader, and the story doesn't stop upon the triumphant return but continues in a messy combination of darkness and light all the way up to David's death and the contested coronation of Bathsheba's son Solomon. It is this no-holds-barred approach to the moral law that leaves us with the truth of the Commandments but also the reality that human nature and human history doesn't follow them. The constant repetition of coveting, stealing, lying, adultery, and murder is in all cultures, and all accounts in various forms that after periods of translation bear a striking similarity regardless of language or other barriers. We are different in many ways but at least the same in our weaknesses. It might be and frankly is tempting to merely discard these boundaries and look for different, more simple guidelines.

Say everything is relative, and you just try to do the best you can. This seems like survival at the point of adolescent frustration in all of us that may look like what it is. However, the adolescent has one advantage of sincerity that most adults just can't claim. On a deeper, more honest level, we know that relative things belong to relative categories like beauty, taste in food, and music. Of course, those things are relative. Who in their right mind would argue that our taste in chocolate is truly superior to a culture that prefers the taste of vanilla? Such examples carry no real weight and don't raise the question of how certain boundaries crossed cause real damage no matter where you live. For example, students have raised the point of an ancient culture's polygamist as an example of cultural relativity. This is an odd example, but it has shown up multiple times, so I merely answer the question of adultery in such a setting as still based on faithfulness within the married relationship.

MOVING FORWARD, WRAPPING UP

In other words, you can have multiple wives or in a few cultures multiple husbands and again go outside the committed boundaries and cheat.

In such cases, the real issue, though it bears further study, is not the number of faithful relationships but the need to be faithful in those relationships. The second step is to ask the student, as I have, if it seems problematic to keep the type of commitment marriage entails with multiple people. Oddly enough, many people who wish to dismiss the commandments as bygone boundaries are quick to point out polygamy within the Bible. Such accusations don't seem to look at the narratives with the Hebrew Bible, which demonstrate over and over that polygamy is an impossible endeavor. Not once in the Jewish scripture is there an example of a happy polygamous relationship. The husband usually looks helpless, and the women and children are viciously competitive. David and Bathsheba are the stories many know from the Hebrew scriptures, but David's harem leads to incest, rape, and murder as well as multiple overthrow attempts by David's sons.

A former colleague of mine once grew very annoyed with me for questioning the discarding of twins in the novel *Things Fall Apart*.[2] She insisted that because it was part of the culture, we had no right to judge it. I argued that people in the novel itself questioned it, and I have met people from that culture who despised the practice. (I knew they would be disregarded in her opinion because they had converted to Christianity.) However, later in the teaching of the book, she was very critical of abusive masculinity in the beating of wives in the book. This was inconsistent with her previous defense of infanticide because the overbearing husband was a product of the culture and couldn't be blamed on colonialism. Why defend one thing and condemn another? The truth is that cultural differences exist but giving up the right to judge something as wrong because it isn't your culture is either misguided or intellectually lazy. It would have been just as easy to find ways in which we discard children in our own culture and thereby realize that not caring for the helpless is part of the dark side of

2. Achebe, Chinua. *Things Fall Apart*.

human nature and one of the most apparent universal abuses of power. "Thou shalt not murder" isn't some uptight boundary. It is evident in all cultures, and the greater mistake would be to pick and choose based on white colonial guilt rather than an honest appraisal of universal weakness and in the case of *Things Fall Apart* a clear disdain for indigenous life in all cases and not just specific customs.

So, if a relative approach to moral boundaries is usually some sort of an excuse system, what is the adult path toward both boundaries and the crossing of them? One last example from my years of teaching rises to this question with an undeniable force. Arthur Miller's *The Crucible* seems to gather and lose fans relative to the teacher's preference. For years, it stood behind his *Death of a Salesman* as the lesser taught of the two great plays. Perhaps it was the movie version that revived its popularity or maybe it's our cultural propensity to be fascinated with the term "witch hunt." For whatever reason, it has had a small revival, and I turn to it as my final examined text regarding the commandments and their effect on human nature.

Looking at John Proctor might seem to be the same old, same old obsession over adultery, but a closer look will show that isn't quite the case. The witch trials themselves were historically not about sexual boundaries but rather selfishness and greed, as exemplified by a land grab. So it seems that theft and coveting are just as dangerous and maybe more so than our assumptions about sex that leads to violence. Miller in his preface to the play says that upon reading the records of the actual John Proctor, he was sure he had bedded the help—namely, Abigail Wilson. He says he knew by experience, so he seems to give some sort of confession and some sort of projection on his interpretation of the facts.[3] In reality, the description of Proctor leaves him more as a mean-spirited boss who may have slapped around the help, and Abigail Wilson seems far too young to be the seductress she is in the play. The adults in the historical records seem plenty greedy, and that is what

---

3. Zoladz, Lindsay. Mailyn and Miller: Star Crossed Misfits. theringer.com March 19, 2018.

probably lead to the hysteria, false accusations, and eventually murder. However, Miller's portrayal, although historically lacking, definitely shows the dark side of human nature regarding breaking the Commandments and also the gut-wrenching kind of confession as the counter to a life that can't seem to live without crossing moral boundaries.

John Proctor is the protagonist, but his relationships are what makes the play so compelling. Unlike what might seem visible, Abigail, the girl Proctor commits adultery with, is not the main focus of the play. She is an aggressive temptation, even resorting to witchcraft to try and curse John Proctor's wife. She, however, is not a hinge but rather a wrench in how the wheel of life should turn. Proctor is a man who means well but falls to seduction and also a sense of what seems like boredom or even distance regarding his relationships. Abigail taunts him and drives the town into a witch-fearing frenzy. However, it is the townspeople's greed and bitterness that make them vulnerable. Witchcraft allows them an excuse to participate openly in bearing false witness, coveting, and even murdering, though it is all under the guise of justice. The final conversation between Elizabeth and John Proctor opens up something beyond the broken boundaries. The scene reads:

> ELIZABETH, *upon a heaving sob that always threatens*: John, it comes to naught that I should forgive you if you'll not forgive yourself. (*Now he turns away a little, in great agony.*) It is not my soul, John, it is yours. (*He stands, as though in physical pain, slowly rising to his feet with a great immortal longing to find his answer. It is difficult to say, and she is on the verge of tears.*) Only be sure of this, for I know it now: Whatever you will do, it is a good man does it. (*He turns his doubting, searching gaze upon her.*) I have read my heart this three month, John. (*Pause.*) I have sins of my own to count. It needs a cold wife to prompt lechery.
>
> PROCTOR, *in great pain:* Enough, enough—
>
> ELIZABETH, *now pouring out her heart*: Better you should know me!

PROCTOR: I will not hear it! I know you!

ELIZABETH: You take my sins upon you, John—

PROCTOR, *in agony*: No, I take my own, my own!

ELIZABETH: John, I counted myself so plain, so poorly made, no honest love could come to me! Suspicion kissed you when I did; I never knew how I should say my love. It were a cold house I kept! (*In fright, she swerves, as Hathorne enters.*)

HATHORNE: What say you, Proctor? The sun is soon up.

Proctor, his chest heaving, stares, turns to Elizabeth. She comes to him as though to plead, her voice quaking.

ELIZABETH: Do what you will. But let none be your judge. There be no higher judge under Heaven than Proctor is! Forgive me, forgive me, John—I never knew such goodness in the world! (*She covers her face, weeping.*)

Proctor turns from her to Hathorne; he is off the earth, his voice hollow.

PROCTOR: I want my life. (IV.204–214)[4]

John Proctor does not confess but, with his wife's forgiveness, finds the courage to stand and hang despite being guiltless of the charge of witchcraft. It is interesting to note that the play ends with Reverend Hale, the expert on all things witchcraft, trying to convince Elizabeth to go to her husband and get him to give a false confession to live. He tells her it may be that because life is God's greatest gift he may hold it a lesser sin to lie. Elizabeth, like a modern-day Eve, answers him that his logic sounds devilish. Where the play ends, the film adds one last scene taken from the historical account. John Proctor, Martha Corey, and Rebekah Nurse stand on the gallows about to hang and break out in the Lord's prayer. The film ends powerfully, with only the taut noose on the screen right after the words, "For thine is the kingdom and

---

4. Miller, Arthur. *The Crucible*. archive.org/strem/TheCrucibleFullText/

the power and the glory forever, amen." It's this ending that brings up what many, over my years of teaching, may want but are kept from, not only by systemic or family issues but also by their world view. The adolescent in all of us wants to bend the rules or make allowances for themselves that they won't give to others. However, in general, when confronted with their shortcomings, the individual will either resort to excusing their actions or be temporarily or lastingly crushed by the shaming process. Technology has not alleviated this darker side of human nature. John Proctor's conversation with his wife is key to looking at forgiveness not so much in a transactional sense of this for that but in the sense of his wife's offering him forgiveness by acknowledging her weakness. It could be seen as letting him off the hook for his affair, but his immediate turning against her admission shows his ownership, not in excusing his past behavior but in refusing to blame her. It is the kind of risky confession that could be called a leap of faith but is instead a simple act of surrender lacking the force of a leap but still holding the same vulnerability. This sort of intimacy is what the adolescent in all of us wants but perhaps without the risk. The adolescent response would be a confession with conditions. The kind of admission that calls for a confession from the victim, a qualifier that not only admits but explains why the crossing of boundaries was necessary in the first place, reduces any crossing of moral boundaries to a sort of misunderstanding. In this, we are all adolescents, and our relativism in looking down at archaic commandments comes from a combination of fear and pride. Fear at being exposed to and pride in excusing our behavior.

 Now the fear of exposure is even more immediate, and that is why I brought up technology. Today's smart technology brings shame to those who have done nothing wrong and shame to those who are guilty. Social media may bring some injustices to light, but its sparks are so quick that they can start a forest fire of shaming in seconds. John Proctor goes to court and confesses his affair to save his wife. His wife lies to cover for him knowing all too well what the loss of his good name would mean in the community. Today, the reality that false accusations can both be leveled without proof and without even a person's knowledge of being accused creates a virtual pillory. The rage of teenagers and adults who turn on each other in today's society makes the witch-hunting crazed mobs of *The Crucible* and the mean-spirited Puritan women of *The Scarlet Letter* look tame and measured. David Brooks in his column, titled "The Cruelty of Call Out Culture"[5] discusses the phenomenon of the call-out culture. He refers to an NPR podcast titled "Invisibilia" most recently interviewing two people involved in the online cultural custom of calling people out.

The first example is of a punk band that has a gig canceled because one of the band members has been accused of sending inappropriate texts to a woman at the location of the latest show. The band dismisses the accusations, but the female member of the band stews and, upon arriving home, denounces her band mate online. It works, and he leaves the band, the punk community, and, presumably, the area itself. The band mate who denounced him has no regrets but runs into the same process when she is outed by old pictures of her mocking a classmate in what appears to be a pattern of bullying. She does not deny them and suffers the same exile from her band and community. She accepts the shaming and says she feels like a monster. The author, Brooks, questions whether a society can move forward when its primary mode of social warning and boundary making is a shame. John Proctor, when confessing to the court to save his wife, argues his sincerity by asking what man would throw away his good name? His confession contradicts his wife's cover, but his refusal to confess witchcraft is his final condemnation. It is his willingness to make a moral stand that breaks the cycle of shame that was based on actual adultery. The confession will free his soul if not his body. Like Hawthorne's Dimmesdale, scaffold confession will cost him his life. The scenes seem extreme to the modern viewer. Surely the point is not to be so religious and extreme? Everything in moderation moves us away from such shaming? However, everyone who thoughtfully considers this knows that shame hasn't disappeared. The reality

---

5. Brooks, David. "The cruelty of call out culture." *New York Times*. January 14, 2019.

of defined moral boundaries isn't the primary issue. The truth is that boundaries measured relatively tend to bring about absolute shame. Boundaries measured more absolutely bring more relative shame and punishment. The commandment to not murder led to definitions of murder so that we have inherited degrees of guilt, manslaughter, and degrees of murder. We differentiate between grand theft, larceny, and shoplifting by having a commandment that says stealing is wrong. However, online, with today's adolescents and frankly so many adults, there is no redemption, only simple labels. Once condemned on the pillory of social media, one cannot be forgiven. Perhaps groups can forgive, but those are just the acceptance of the tribal distinctions that existed before the shaming began. The Commandments are boundaries that reflect human nature and what happens to people when they cross boundaries or the necessary barriers for healthy living, what the ancient Hebrew scriptures called freedom.

I close not with another literary example or article but rather an example from my classroom, a place where I have spent countless hours of my life. The presentation was over the novel *The Kite Runner*, and the student giving it was one of the brightest and, without question, the most widely read student I have ever taught. The presentation was solid, but the most memorable statement was the argument she built over stating that the principal antagonist, a vicious young man named Assef had lost his humanity as a result of a brutal sexual assault on a younger boy and a life of pedophilia. The point was made forcefully but concluded with the proviso that she realized that everyone makes their moral systems. After what was a fairly anemic response to her presentation during the allotted question and answer period, we wrapped up the class just before the bell rang to end the period. The next day during an overview of all the presentations I asked her why she had pulled her punch at the end of the presentation. She seemed puzzled, so I explained that she had built a forceful argument demonstrating that the character had given up his very soul in becoming a lifelong predator. The student became emotional, and I let it drop, but she thanked me later for making her look at something differently than she had before. The truth was that her presentation, at least in the condemnation of Assef, had an almost Biblical forcefulness and was what another generation might even have seen as a justification for believing in damnation. However, the qualifying of her argument had the sort of sanitized approach one sees when a student or anyone else attempts to qualify all points and conclusions with tolerance. Why would anyone in their right mind qualify assault or pedophilia? The student certainly did, but at the time we are staying true to a belief system that did not have the moral or linguistic force to condemn real evil. John Proctor nearly loses his faith in the face of his own failed confession and the lies he is almost convinced to confess to. However, it isn't the commandments that condemn him. Bearing false witness is the commandment that isn't stressed in his interrogation because witchcraft is the focus. The lies surrounding the hysteria are tolerated because the system is sustaining itself by its power, which seems dangerously close to both false witnesses and breaking the first commandment. So many times, students have pointed out the flaws of religious injustice, the crusades, the witch trials, and on and on. However, what they put in its place, a vague notion of science, some idea of tolerance, often lacks the moral definitions even to identify real evil, even evil that begs intuitively to be defined and opposed. Do horrible things happen in the world because people are too religious? Are we capable of coming up with better boundaries that lack definition but will somehow keep us from hurting others and ourselves in the endlessly repeated cycles of human frailty and abuse? Proctor's gut-wrenching confession to the court and his wife, along with his wife's admission of weakness to him, points out not a lack of moral law but a weakness in keeping moral boundaries and one final piece of genius, forgiveness. Forgiveness assumes moral boundaries, and anything other than those assumptions and definitions will bring about the sort of excusing we all have graduate degrees in. Without forgiveness, everyone lives with varying degrees of guilt and shame. Denying this, over some time leads to anything from irresponsible behavior to truly damaging lifestyle patterns. The Commandments don't outline the patterns of confession and repentance, but they provide a baseline for why it is necessary. In the end, they are what make us free, but we fall short of freedom, preferring license and excuses with various degrees of complicity. A virtuous life does not end with the Commandments, but it does begin there. Perhaps there was a time when societies accepted this more. To be honest, I really don't know. I know at least that time has not come nor will be my days. I do know, however, that my days and anyone else's are still bound by the challenge of living free. If we can't keep the commands, we show our need for confession, because the boundaries prove over and over not be legitimate. Even our tweaking of them looks feeble, like a weak parody, reflecting the idea with some sort of bent application, which makes us feel better about ourselves but doesn't remove the natural consequences that come from crossing ancient boundaries. In John Proctor, Arthur Dimmesdale, Langston Hughes's old woman, and Amir's self-assessment, we see a need for repentance. Our adolescent selves cringe at being outed. If we're honest, our adult selves are even more afraid. Clear moral boundaries not only show us the faults of others and our society, but they show us our own moral detours and border crossings. It is, of course, easier to point out others flaws or to try to come up with another system of established boundaries that isn't so telling. All the refiguring and finger-pointing doesn't keep the mirror away in the moments when life becomes painful. The moral law doesn't provide forgiveness or second chances; it simply and clearly points out the need for such realities that brings us to the end of ourselves quite quickly. In the end, the positive aspects of the Commandments are inferred by opposites. Only when the sign says do not enter or points out that the road is a dead end can the motorist turn around. How far the lost traveler can go before a U-turn makes no difference is another matter for another book. Most likely such a work is for a sharper mind and a keener writing skill than me. Nonetheless, yesterday, today, and tomorrow, we will always need wrong way signs not only to acknowledge such paths but also to help us turn and to help us help others turn back the right way. And, in the moments of our story where we are the Dimmesdales and John Proctors we also need the boundaries to measure how great forgiveness can be. However, that is another book for another time.

Afterword

SERIOUS thoughts come from multiple sources even when they have a singular focus. I was fortunate to have a mother who continually read the scriptures and read them regularly with us, not really glossing over the difficult parts. My father would have preferred the references to avoiding prostitutes and other less than savory passages to be read at an older age, but his skepticism and love of formality in church has also been a part of me taking the scripture seriously when I like it, and when it is puzzling to me. To my sister and brother-in-law, Janet and Mark, I owe an enormous debt at their ability to live out their faith in their community and to their loyalty to me, especially during times of doubt and loss. To my longtime friends Mike and Eric, I owe a debt of brotherhood for long talks late into the night, Facebook messages and texts as we have all gone from being young and single to older fathers and husbands. To my wife and sons, I owe more than words can express, for their connection to me, their enjoyment of me as a person and their loyalty despite my many flaws. Lastly, I would be remiss to not mention my place of work, specifically the IB classes at Smithfield Selma High School. If one of my students from the last few years were to peruse these pages, they would see an overwhelming amount of my junior and senior class content. No, I don't teach at a Christian school nor do I lead any type of Christian club, but the literature I referenced throughout this book is ultimately from my learning lab, the upstairs class at a medium-sized public school in Smithfield, North Carolina.

www.ingramcontent.com/pod-product-compliance
Lightning Source LLC
Chambersburg PA
CBHW070321100426
42743CB00011B/2509